In Finding Him
I Found Me

IN FINDING HIM I FOUND ME

A TESTIMONY OF HEALING AND DELIVERANCE

Dr. Bessie Stewart-Banks

Conscious of the Heart Publishing, LLC

IN FINDING HIM I FOUND ME by Bessie Stewart-Banks

Published by Conscious of the Heart Publishing, LLC
P.O. Box 1452
Redan, Georgia 30074

No parts of this book may be reproduced, scanned, stored, or transmitted in any form by any means without written permission. Please preserve the authors' rights and purchase only authorized editions.

Unless otherwise indicated, all Scripture quotations are taken from the Holy Bible, New Living Translation, copyright © 1996, 2004, 2007, 2013, 2015 by Tyndale House Foundation. Used by permission of Tyndale House Publishers, Inc., Carol Stream, Illinois 60188. All rights reserved.

Scripture quotations marked (NIV) are taken from the Holy Bible, New International Version®, NIV®. Copyright © 1973, 1978, 1984, 2011 by Biblica, Inc.™ Used by permission of Zondervan. All rights reserved worldwide. www.zondervan.com The "NIV" and "New International Version" are trademarks registered in the United States Patent and Trademark Office by Biblica, Inc.™

Scripture taken from the New King James Version®. Copyright © 1982 by Thomas Nelson. Used by permission. All rights reserved.

Scripture quotations marked KJV are from the King James Version of the Bible.

This book was designed with the intent of only providing information based on the life experiences of the author. The author nor publisher shall have no liability or responsibility to any person or persons regarding harm or loss that may occur directly or indirectly by the information contained there within.

Copyright @2017 Bessie Stewart-Banks
Cover design: Dimitrinka Cvetkoski (www.peacockdesign.pro)

Author's photo: Michael Johnson of Abstract Perceptions Creative Photography

All rights reserved

ISBN-13 978-0692888001
ISBN-10 069288004

Library of Congress Control Number 2017908110

Printed in the United States of America

DEDICATION

This book is dedicated to my sons, Eric and Jeston. It has been an honor and a privilege that God trusted me enough to raise you both, only He knew what I would have to endure but I must say it has been worth it. Thank you so much for not only being obedient children but for allowing God to use you to touch my life.

To my mother, Mildred, thank you for always being there for me and being the rock that has kept our family together through all of our highs and lows. I love you and may our Heavenly Father bless you with many more years of life, health, and strength. It would be remiss of me to not acknowledge my father, the late Easton (a.k.a. "IT"), who exemplified the qualities of a real man; who took great joy and pride in taking care of his children. Your turtle frog loves and misses you.

Special thanks to someone I consider to be my spiritual mother, Mrs. Arletha White, a woman who has truly taught me what it is to be a Proverbs 31 Woman of God. Thank you for sharing with me some of your most intimate life experiences and speaking into my life at a time when I thought I would not make it. I would like to this time as well to acknowledge my older siblings: Steven, Leroy, Audrea, Arrelin "Net", Alesia, Freddie, Christy and Terry for inspiring me in your own unique and special way.

Special recognition also goes to someone who is more like a sister to me than a cousin... Monica Tellis. Thank you for your prayers and the many times you stood as a sounding board for me in the airing of my grievances in life.

To my beloved pastor and spiritual leader Apostle, Bishop Eddie L. Long (gone but not forgotten) and to his lovely wife, First Lady Elder Vanessa Long; I thank you both for allowing the Lord to use you to touch the lives of His people throughout the world. Your spirits have resonated in such a way that every time you have spoken, it was and still is in sync with what the Holy Spirit has already imparted into me. The anointing that was placed on the life of Bishop Long and continues to rest on Elder Vanessa Long has truly been a blessing to those who have come and will come into your presence.

Many thanks goes out to those individuals I did not mention by name (you know who you are) who made a profound impact on my life, whether it was personally or professionally.

Most of all, I give honor, glory and praise to the One and Only True Living God, Elohim. Thank you for bringing me to this point of spiritual maturity, where I can share with others what you have brought me through and what you are making me to be.

ACKNOWLEDGEMENTS

My sincere thanks to Jeremy Collin for his editing service and ensuring that every "I" was dotted and every "T" was crossed and that an excellent piece of literary work was produced. Thank you to Dimitrinka Cvetkoski, the creative designer at Peacock Design for assisting me in bringing the vision of my book cover into fruition. Thank you also goes to a friend of a friend, Associate Minister, Reverend Danielle Alyce Rome-Briggs at Springfield Baptist Church in Raleigh, North Carolina, for the composition of such an awesome Foreword. Thank you, thank you and many blessings to you and your family! Finally, thank you to photographer Michael Johnson of Abstract Perceptions Creative Photography for his professionalism and workmanship.

FOREWORD

Spiritually engaging and emotionally revealing- these descriptors begin to inform the audience of the nature of this testimonial penned by Dr. Bessie Stewart-Banks. It commences at a place where many Christians have found themselves, a place of cavernous emotional pain. It is this pain that brought Bessie to the point of truly experiencing the loving, affirming, and merciful nature of God.

The reality of pain is that it takes on a life of its own, taking those who endure it on journeys to depression, isolation, hatred, and faithlessness. The questions that arose from the abyss of pain took Bessie to a very dark place on her faith walk. She found herself in a place many of us have also ventured through our own pain, the place where God's existence, his nature and his wisdom are all questioned.

This is the beginning of this testimony, the questions that led to a far deeper knowledge and relationship with God. Each chapter is intensely personal and teeming with spiritual nuggets that are demonstrative of phases of the Christian journey.

Bessie's journey becomes a mirror through which we can more clearly see our own Christian journey. We question the existence and nature of God, pursue intimate knowledge of God, hunger for a relationship with God, are transformed by the Word of God, grow in the Grace of God, build our faith in God, become enlightened by the truth of God, then we are emboldened by a growing confidence in God, and become discerning by the wisdom of God. This text is breathed upon by the Holy Spirit and is enlivened throughout by The Living Word of God.

The culmination of this testimony is a beautifully stirring exhortation for readers. Be assured that as you take this journey through the pages of this testimony you will grow in your faith. Each step rings true the greatest truth being the word that is beautifully inspiring and life-affirmingly interwoven throughout its pages.

I offer this prayer as you begin your journey with this awe inspiring testimony, Jeremiah 29:11(KJV) - "For I know the thoughts that I think toward you, saidth the Lord, thoughts of peace, and not of evil, to give you an expected end."

May this revelation of God's power reach even the depths of your pain, restore your relationship with God in the midst of true dismay, and redeem you from faithlessness. May the Holy Spirit both comfort and empower you to embark upon this Christian journey with your eyes and your heart open to the joy of the Lord. It is, after all, only possible to know oneself through a true knowledge of the Holy God.

Bibliography of Rev. Danielle Alyce Rome-Briggs

Rev. Danielle Alyce Rome-Briggs is an Associate Minister at Springfield Baptist Church in Raleigh, North Carolina and has spent many years serving under the leadership of the late Pastor Daniel Sanders. She has authored two books of poetry, Another Day's Journey and From Marah to Elim: Poetic Journeys through Scripture for Christians. She also conducted an interview with world renowned poet Sonia Sanchez that has been widely published in numerous critical publications.

"Change is not change until you decide to change"--If you are ready for a change then this book is for you. Get ready for a journey that will change the course of your life. Ready, Set, Read!

Dr. Bessie Stewart-Banks

CONTENTS

ACKNOWLEDGEMENTS vii
FOREWORD viii
PREFACE xiv
    The Question xiv
CHAPTER ONE 1
    The Dark Room 1
CHAPTER TWO 10
    Tainted Pursuits 10
CHAPTER THREE 19
    Spiritual Famine 19
CHAPTER FOUR 27
    Spiritual Transformation 27
CHAPTER FIVE 35
    Point of Spiritual Growth 35
CHAPTER SIX 44
    Building of Relentless Faith 44
CHAPTER SEVEN 56
    Destiny Realized 56
CHAPTER EIGHT 60
    A Champion is Born 60
CHAPTER NINE 66
    Lessons Learned Along the Way 66

CHAPTER TEN	83
Author's Prayer	83
SPIRITUAL GROWTH GUIDE FOR CHANGE	87
Appendix A	88
Appendix B	95

Preface
The Question

Have you ever had a turning point in your life where you lost your footage in the path you were traveling, your faith in God, and his word as well as stopped believing and seeking His face and questioned why you were even born? Well, I have and my journey began when I was about fourteen years old around the time I lost my father.

As a child of a single mother I always felt different from everyone else. I am the only child my parents had together. Both my mother and father had children respectively from previous marriages, totaling eight siblings for me. Being born in this type of family demographics, I never felt like I belonged anywhere and this feeling became more evident when I was in the eighth grade in Junior High School. This period of time is so profound in my memory because this is the year my father passed away due to complications from lupus and diabetes.

Before his death I was a mild, meek and quiet person (some would say I was a bit shy). As a result of my father's death I became more introverted, I drew more away from people and was at a point that I felt angry at the world, those who were around me (mostly my family) and even at God. I did not understand it at the time but my father's death started the process of shaping me into the person I am today.

"For those who find me find life and receive favor from the Lord"

-Proverbs 8:35(NLT)

CHAPTER ONE

The Dark Room

*"You watched me as I was being formed in utter seclusion,
As I was woven together in the dark womb"*
Psalm 139:15 (NIV)

The Journey Begins. It was April 2nd and during this period of time my father was spending his second stint in the hospital for complications due to lupus and diabetes. I never knew how debilitating lupus and diabetes could be on the human body, but I experienced it firsthand from my father's ongoing battle with both diseases. As a result of my father enduring years of living with lupus and diabetes he lost his eyesight, the ability to walk and eventually I believe his will to live.

At this very moment you may be saying to yourself what significance does this have on this story? Well, let me explain my father and I had a regime where we would call each other every morning and say, *"I love you and have a good day."* However, on this particular day I was not able to reach him on the telephone. I made several attempts but to no avail. After being unsuccessful at reaching him at the hospital I decided that I would try again once I arrived at school. I was fortunate in those days because as part of my nine week rotation of courses I was able to work in the school office. Nevertheless, once I arrived at school I called the hospital again and this time a nurse answered the telephone, as I proceeded to ask for my father she informed me that he was unavailable to speak with me and that I needed to contact my mother. I thought to myself, *"Why do I need to contact my mother?"*

I gave no further thought to what the nurse said to me and attempted to call my mother at home before she left to go to work. Upon calling my mother, I discovered that there was no one at home because the phone rang several times with no answer. After not being able to reach anyone on the phone I became concerned and wondered to myself, *"What's going on to today, no one wants to answer their telephone?"* Up to this point I had no knowledge that my father had already passed away and that was the reason why I couldn't reach anyone. Needless to say, I continued to make several attempts to reach someone on the phone at home and finally someone did answered and it was my sister's boyfriend. As I inquired about where my mother was, he blurted out to me, *"Your mom is not at home and your dad is dead!"* I thought to myself this has to be a continuous of April fool's jokes and I told him *"to stop playing with me and put my mom on the phone."* Suddenly, I heard my sister in the background ask him, *"Why did you say that to her?"*

By this time I was in a state of shock and disbelief from what I had just heard. I dropped the telephone and one of the school secretaries' rushed over to me and questioned me as to what happened. At the same time, another secretary picked up the telephone and was informed by my sister that my father had just passed away. I could not speak and from this I was sent to the nurses' station to be comforted by school staff and administration. Nothing they said to me mattered or even made an impact on my feelings at that moment. While all of this was transpiring my mother had already been informed of my father's death and she was on her way to the school to pick me up.

Several moments had passed before my mother arrived at the school. Upon her arrival, school staff escorted her to the nurses' station where I was. When I saw her, I immediately began to scream and cry out *"why, why did he have to die!"* My mother consoled me until I calmed down and was able to leave the school. I was so physically and emotionally drained from the devastating news of my father's death that I had to be wheeled out to my mother's car in a wheelchair. Thusly, when mother and I arrived home I was so angry at the way I was informed of my father's death that I hated everyone around me at the time. I know the word *"hate"* is a strong connotation of an expression but can you blame me, no one wants to find out as a joke that a love one has passed away.

Nevertheless, days had passed and my family finalized the plans for my father's funeral. I remember those days just like it was yesterday. Family members came from all over Florida and Georgia to attend my father's funeral and I was surprise to see how many relatives he had. There were people who would come up to me and tell me what a good man he was but every word they spoke sound like someone speaking inside a tunnel. I literally walked around during this period of time like a zombie and nothing that was said to me could erase the pain of sadness I was experiencing.

The day I dreaded the most had arrived, the day my father was laid to rest. The funeral was a sad but jovial occasion because for a split moment I was able to forget that my father was no longer with us due to the many stories that family members and friends shared about his life. However, that was short lived when different singers' began to sing sad spiritual songs and that only took me back to a sad state yet again. Subsequently, my father's funeral lasted nearly three and a half hours before we made it to the burial site.

Needless to say, shortly after the funeral, my family and I returned to my father's house and prepared for the repast. By this time it had been a long day and I did not want to be around people anymore, so I decided to go into my father's room and stare out the window like he and I did so many times. As I sat on the side of the bed in my father's tiny bedroom apartment so many unexplained questions rushed through my mind.

One particular question came to mind, a typical question that people ask of God when they lose a love one: *Why did he have to die?* The other question that I had no answer to at the time was: *Why are we born just to die?* Unsuspectingly, a close family friend overheard me utter those words and came into the room to offer me some comfort. She said to me that God knows what we can handle and my father could no longer handle the illness that his body had succumbed to.

Being a child and not all the way a true believer in Jesus Christ, I found no solace in the words she was speaking to me. All I knew was that I lost my father at a time when I needed him the most. My sister and brothers from his previous marriage had the chance to spend all of their childhood, teen and young adulthood years with him and all I thought to myself was, *Why not me?* I thought it was unfair that my siblings had a chance to spend all those years with our father and I only had a short time with him. As I reflect on those times, I know it was selfish of me to think that way because there are countless people who would love to spend the amount of quality time I was able to have with my father and the fond memories of him that are stored in my memory bank.

Nonetheless, after my father's death family and friends alike dissipated and were seldom heard from again. A year had passed and I was still in search of an answer to the question that was pondering in my mind: *Why did my father have to die?* So I decided to attend church with the intent of finding the answer. After about six months of attending church I got baptized with the assumption that the feelings I had from my father's death would somehow mysteriously disappear. There was one problem, however, with this thought process and it was I did not have a personal relationship with Jesus Christ. Additionally, I was not serious and not fully committed to the spiritual shifting that would take place. I have discovered, now that I am older and more knowledgeable of the word of God, that getting baptized was just one factor toward understanding why things happen the way they do in our lives.

Beyond the scope of discovering why my father had to die, I felt as if I didn't belong anywhere and the type of family I was born into did not help matters. Being the only child that my parents had together, I often felt a sense of alienation from my sisters and brothers on both sides. Despite the fact I was raised to view my siblings as my sisters and brothers with no regard to half- sister or half- brother, I still did not feel accepted; and at times I felt uncomfortable being around them because each set of my siblings respectively shared the same biological parent. It's hard for a child to accept and believe that they are cherished and welcomed in a family where the children have different parents. I am certainly aware that in today's society where blended families are now viewed as the new norm that may not be the case. For clarification, the dynamics of blended families maybe inclusive of:

couples with children from other relationships, grandparents raising grandchildren, aunts or uncles raising their siblings' children for one reason or another. No matter how you clarify a families' composition, the feelings of alienation and loneliness can still exist for a child due to their family's circumstance.

I truly believe that the feelings of alienation I had as a young child was one of the major reasons why I oftentimes kept to myself. I was under the assumption that people around me could relate to my feelings of alienation. I would find out later in life that this train of thought was false, especially, when a person does not come from a similar place as you and has not experienced some of the things you have in life; it's hard for them to identify with your feelings. Subsequently, the anger I felt from my father's death I harbored for many years all the way up until I was about nineteen years old and was heading off to college. My college years were an expressive time for me, a period of time when I began to be extroverted and outgoing.

My course of self-discovery during this period of time in my life was somewhat atrocious to the point that I displayed a rebellious attitude toward my mother and other family members. There is an incident in particular that occurred between one of my sisters' and me. This was the same sister whose boyfriend told me that my father had died. She had come home to visit for the summer and on several occasions we got into heated arguments over the simplest things. I got to the point where I would ignore her and pretend as if she didn't exist. I don't recall the exact words that were used during our arguments but I am sure the words that were spoken were not polite or pleasant.

Little did I know that the arguments I had with my sister stemmed from unresolved feelings I had because of my father's death. I used my sister and mother as an escape goat to lash out my pain, frustration, anger, feelings of abandonment and rejection. Even though years had passed since the death of my father I couldn't shake off the feelings that were festering in my spirit. The displaced anger I exhibited back then was because I did not understand the disease that my father died from, I did not quite comprehend the concept of death and I didn't understand how to apply the word of God for comfort nor did anyone else seem to know how to either.

My anger, feelings of bitterness and abandonment were further perpetuated in the way I treated people and the way in which I spoke. According to Proverbs 18:21(NLT): *"the tongue can bring death or life; those who love to talk will reap the consequences."* Because of my inability to communicate and effectively express myself, I would sometimes speak whatever I was feeling at the time. Oftentimes, I did not care if the words I spoke hurt someone's feelings and it was seldom that I would apologize. Also, if a person asked me a question I was very callous and indignant in my response to them.

Eventually, my failure to express myself in an effective way and the ill-treatment of people lead me to a destructive and promiscuous lifestyle. No one, not even my closest friends at the time knew the life I was living because I projected a persona that was representative of an innocent, nerdy, and quiet person. While at the same time I would be involved with various young men, of which none of them knew about the other one. From this assertion you can say I was living a double life, at one moment as Doctor Jekyll and another moment as Mr. Hyde; leading those in close proximity to me to believe that I was one way, when in fact I was another. Although, it's hard for me to openly admit that this is the type of behavior I once dabbled in; it is necessary because my past lifestyle will help someone else come to terms with the way they are living.

More than often, when we regardless of our age, race, educational or socio-economic background, do not know how to properly address certain issues that arise in our life and we do not have anyone to turn to for guidance we tend to subject ourselves to unscrupulous living in spite of the consequences. The unscrupulous living I'm referring to is so detrimental to the point it leads some people down the road where their mental state and physical well-being is placed in jeopardy. Some may people get hooked on drugs, while others may contract deadly diseases because of their promiscuous ways. Meanwhile, other people may become involved in abusive relationships and due to fear they can't find a way of escape. In the end, some people don't live long enough to share their story of how they made it through their storm of adversity. Whatever, the case may be, the choice a person makes due to the lack of support they may or may not receive from family or friends can have a negative or positive impact on the direction of that person's life.

I publicly confess that it was by God's grace and mercy that I did not contract any deadly disease, experiment with any type of drug and did not get involve with an abusive man. I know that it was God who was shielding me from the snares of this world as well as protecting me from myself. It is amazing to me how God loves and cares for his children so much that he will cover them during their time of ignorance and disobedience. There are people right now in today's society who are experiencing some of the same scenarios I have just described. Could it be you? If you have identified with any of the illustrations from my life thus far please know and understand that there is a lesson in the midst of your pain and those lessons learned, no matter how unimaginable the pain was or is; they are significant to your growth and purpose. As I have matured over time, I have discovered that I was longing for the love and attention that I once received from my father. I learned that the love and attention that I desired was only going to be found in the development of a personal relationship with God and his son Jesus Christ. I don't denounce the bond I had with my earthly father but I find it to be true that this relationship was temporary, for I truly belong to God. It was God's will to use my father to get me here on earth to fulfill His will. I will always love and miss my dad and with the reassurance of salvation, I will one day see him again in heaven. For this reason, it doesn't matter what type of family I was born into but what really matters is that I was born.

Despite the fact that my early years as a young adult were dishonorable and shameful because of the behavior I showed toward my mother, family members and myself; they are part of my formative years and cannot be erased. I can only learn from them and strive to do better and improve as an individual. Many times we fail to realize that the things we endure in our childhood and young adulthood years are points for shaping not only our character but also our faith. I am captivated as to how God through his infinite wisdom knows beforehand what we will experience in life; well before we arrived here in this distant land we call Earth. Although, some of my experiences I have revealed to you are minor in perspective they are profound in my development. Please do not take it likely for what I have just shared with you about the first few years of my life. These trials were only the stepping-stones used to usher me into the dark room to be processed.

CHAPTER TWO

Tainted Pursuits

*"And what do you benefit if you gain the whole
world but lose your own soul?"*
Mark 8:36 (NLT)

It is one thing to live a life in secret but another to live a life chasing after things that add no value to your existence. Many of the things that we strive to obtain and accomplish in life are done because we think it will make us feel important, better about ourselves or more acceptable. However, we fail to understand that our quest to gain love, acceptance and influence along with monetary and materialistic possessions are actually tainted pursuits filled with false realities. For definition purposes, tainted pursuits entail things that people chase after that are deemed dangerous, harmful to one's own well-being and essentially causes the person to do things that they normally would not do.

Majority of the things we tend to pursue in life inadvertently cloud our vision and create distractions. These pursuits often diminish our perception about life, our identity, our purpose and the direction in which we are headed in life. In addition, tainted pursuits destroy our hopes and dreams, our peace and joy, our soundness of mind and our creative ability. Consequently, pursuits without true meaning often open the door to corruptible thinking, bad decision making, and poor choices in every facet of our lives.

Ultimately, tainted pursuits lead us to become involved in unhealthy relationships and being people pleasers. Unhealthy relationships and being people pleasers with the exception of drugs and sexual immorality are two of the most obstructive traps that an individual can be enslaved by. For instance, once you are involved in a relationship with a person you know is not a good fit for you and where you are headed in life; you can't get rid of them. For whatever reason, that person latches onto you like a leech and no matter what you do you can't shake them; they won't leave out of your life.

On the flip side of that notion, once you start appeasing others and fulfilling the hopes and dreams they have set for your life you become lured into a vicious cycle of pleasing people. The cycle of pleasing people only leads to putting what you desire and what you want out of life on the backburner in order to fulfill the goals that person has envisioned for you to accomplish.

Seemingly, you will always seek the approval of others for every move you make in life not realizing that God made you capable of making decisions about your life. As a result of this cycle of behavior you will live a miserable, unhappy and unfulfilled life. There are many other deadly traps that can easily draw us into living a deceitful life such as chasing after money and cars. Money and cars seem to be the two main factors that attract people. Oftentimes, the desire to obtain certain comforts in life cause some people to do any and everything in order to gain them; never understanding that material things will never fill the void they have in life.

In today's society many people become enticed by the images they view in advertisements and music videos not realizing that the objective of companies is to utilize subliminal messages to capture the attention of their viewers. Unfortunately, those same individuals who viewed the music videos and advertisements become so intrigued and envious that they begin to believe that they too must have the same item they have seen. Subsequently, the lustfulness of material possessions not only distorts the path we should take but also how we should live life.

The story of Esau and Jacob (Genesis 25:27-34), serves as a good example of someone's desire to have something so bad that they disregard what they must give up in order to have it. Within the context of the story Esau, the eldest son of Isaac's children returned home from a long and tiresome hunting trip. Upon Esau's entering the home of his father, Isaac, he discovered that his brother Jacob had prepared a pot of stew in which he wanted some because he was hungry. Esau insisted that his brother give him some of the stew and Jacob agreed on the condition that he would hand over his birthright as the firstborn, being famished Esau agreed. Unknowingly, Esau not only forfeited his birthright for a bowl of stew but he played a role in opening the door to treachery in his life.

As time progressed Esau was yet again betrayed by the acts of Jacob, which caused Isaac their father to pass his blessings onto the wrong son (Read Genesis 27:1-40). As a result of the greed and the covetousness of one brother over another's rights and privileges, discord and resentment was brought within the family. Based on this biblical illustration of Esau and Jacob, you can see that the desires of one person can have an adverse effect on the other person as well as the future of their interaction and relationship.

Climbing the social ladder to success is another deadly trap that some people get sucked into without them realizing it. Many people in their quest to become successful often feel that if they are in relationship with the right people or connected to the right group of people they will have a better vantage point in accomplishing their goals. The formulation of this notion dates back to the old cliché of: *It's not what you know but who you know.* It is unfortunate, however, for people who think along these lines because not everyone who is business and successful will be open to help them reach their goal.

Moreover, people who desire to become successful in life should not solely rely on being accepted into a prestigious circle of influential people but more so rely on hard work, dedication, wisdom, commitment and trusting in God. By doing so, you eliminate the likelihood of owing someone a favor because they helped you out in fulfilling your vision. I find it to be true based on personal experience that if you pray and seek after God as well as commit your plans to him, he will send the right people in your path to assist you in fulfilling the goals you have set for your life. For it is stated in Jeremiah 17:7(NLT), *"but blessed are those who trust in the Lord and have made the Lord their hope and confidence."* Therefore, we should rely a 100% on God and zero percentage on man.

There was a point in time in my own life when I too lusted after meaningless pursuits that only left me with heartache and disappointment. The pursuits I'm referencing to involved nonsensical relationships. My longing for fatherly love lead me to seek love and affection from any young man who showed me a level of interest; while at the same time ignoring the fact that most of them wanted one thing and one thing only (you can draw your own conclusion). I cared less that I did not receive the compassion and treatment I wanted and deserved. I allowed myself to be treated disrespectfully because I wanted so much to be loved and treated like a princess. My desire caused me to willingly ignore the warning signs that were apparent by the young man's noticeably inappropriate behavior. Not only was I attracted to men who I thought could give me the love I desired but I gravitated to men who I thought I could save. I believe my main objective to a point was to help the men in my life be delivered from their issues.

Sad to say, but I couldn't help anyone with their issues because I had my own issues that I hadn't confronted. For the most part, I was playing a role that was not scripted for me to portray. I did not understand it at the time but my rational for love and affection were valid but the source for which I was seeking them was misguided. There was no way in the world that the men I was involved with were capable of providing me with what I was searching for in life. Consequently, the savior mentality I was walking around with continued until I had a personal encounter with Jesus Christ. My encounter with Jesus was the exact replica of the Samaritan woman at the well.

Based on biblical accounts Jesus was returning from Judea to Galilee (John 4:1-26). While on his long journey back to Galilee Jesus became tired and thirsty because of the noonday heat. As he took a break to rest a Samaritan woman came to the well where he was resting to draw water. Jesus saw what she was doing and asked her to give him some water. The woman was hesitant and confused because it was not custom for Jews and Samaritans to interact with one another. The woman proceeded to ask Jesus why he asked her for a drink. Jesus responded to the woman and said *"If you only knew the gift God has for you and who you are speaking to, you would ask me, and I would give you living water"* (John 4:10, NLT).

From this assertion, the Samaritan woman thought that Jesus was talking about the water in the well but in fact he was talking about salvation. As the conversation between Jesus and the Samaritan woman continued, she asked Jesus to give her the living water that he spoke about. Upon the woman's request Jesus told her to go and get her husband. But the woman said she didn't have a husband and Jesus agreed stating that she had five husbands she was never married to. Jesus further informed the woman that the man she was living with was not her husband either. The conversation between the Samaritan woman and Jesus continued with a series of questions. At the end of the woman's encounter with Jesus, he informed her that he was the Messiah (John 4:26).

Just as Jesus told the woman at well that the water he possesses would quench her thirst, he spoke the same to me. It was clear as day when Jesus told me to stop participating in meaningless relationships with men to whom I was not married to. When Jesus confronted me with the vast details of past my relationships I was appalled by the way in which I had behaved and carried myself.

Nevertheless, I took heed to Jesus' instructions and redirected my focus onto furthering my education and being a single parent. After making such of a proclamation to being a single woman, it was important for me to maintain this type of lifestyle until I felt I had met the right person to bring around my child otherwise it would have been pointless. As time progressed I kept my promise to remain single until I met a young man who would eventually become my husband. When I met this person I thought I had met the man of my dreams, some would say *Mr. Right!*

Overtime, we developed a long distance relationship that lasted for five months before he proposed marriage and I agreed.

Although, he was a great person and possessed some of the qualities that I wanted in a husband; he was not the person for me at that time in my life. We both were immature and had a lot of baggage that we had not unloaded before deciding to commit to a serious relationship. I truthfully ignored all the signs and the questionable cues that were being exhibited by him because I loved him and he loved me. I held onto the premise that *love would conquer all*. Within months of dating we were married and that's when all the problems in our marriage began. Our marriage was tainted from the very beginning because neither one of us had sought God for his approval nor had we confronted the issues of our past. Both of us did not realize it at the time but once we entered into holy matrimony our individual problems became one and doubled in size.

From my perspective, people who are in relationships stand a better chance of survival if they would first commit to dealing with their own issues prior to becoming involved with someone else. I also believe that if dealing with individualized problems requires professional help then those services should be sought after. It is better for that person to get to the root cause of their dysfunction versus walking around living a destructive life and dragging others into their world of calamity. There is one important statement I would like to make concerning counseling and that is by no means does seeking professional counseling deem anyone as crazy nor does it constitute them to be less than a person. On the contrary, counseling helps people to resolve their issues and to become more of a whole person.

Alongside each person dealing with their own personal issues; it is imperative that when two people enter into a relationship with one another and they are thinking about marriage they should ask themselves why they want to be with the other person.

Now that I am older I wish I knew then what I know now, it would have saved me from a lot of headache, heartache, disappointment, and sleepless nights crying.

Moreover, it is suggested that prior to a person entering into a committed relationship with another person they should perform a self-assessment on themselves. Performing self-assessments are not only beneficial for the one who is conducting it on themselves but it is also beneficial for their potential partner. Conducting self-assessments reveals to the individual the particular area or areas in their life that they need to address and correct. Performing self-assessments allows the individual the opportunity to become more in tune with him or herself and discover who they really are and what they really want out of life.

Additionally, self-assessments serve as a conduit to uncovering any hidden personal qualities a person never knew they possessed and it gives them a chance to enhance the qualities they already have knowledge about. In essence, conducting self-assessments on oneself lowers the probability of couples breaking up because they took the time to found out who they were prior to committing to a lifelong relationship.

Although, I allowed myself to be involved in various unproductive relationships and a tumultuous marriage I found out that the love, validation, and affirmation I longed for would never be received from a man. I failed to realize or even understand that these forms of affection were only going to be obtained from God. I also discovered that regardless of the fact that I lived a life that was unbecoming for a young woman or what some people would term as *loose living* I knew I was worthy and that God could one day use me for a greater purpose. Some people would argue that God can't use a person who has lived a life that is less than perfect.

I would argue and say who but God is perfect. I think it is an oxymoron for anyone to think that way. I believe that if God could use Rahab (a harlot/prostitute) to hide and protect two spies sent into Jericho by Joshua a servant of God to spy out the land (Joshua 2:1-24); if God could use a man by the name of Moses who was a murderer (Exodus 2:11-14) and one of Jesus' very own disciples' named Peter who lied three times about his affiliation with him (Matthew 26: 69-75); who's to say that he can't use anyone he chooses for the expansion of his kingdom.

Henceforth, if God could use people like Rahab, Moses, and Peter; how much more could he use you or me for the advancement of his kingdom?

CHAPTER THREE

Spiritual Famine

"........Why do you have so little faith?"
Luke 12:28 (NLT)

Throughout everyone's life there will be moments when they will experience bouts of doubt and confusion, times when they will feel hopeless and find no purpose to living. More than often doubt and confusion arises when people are spiritually detached because of one reason or another. Oftentimes, a person becomes spiritually detached because they have stopped believing in God. Other rationales for a person's spiritual detachment stems from them never being exposed to the word of God, they had a negative religious experience, something horrific happened in their life and they blame God for it or they simply believe that God does not exist. In essence, if we don't have a personal relationship with Jesus Christ and we have no hope, trust, or faith in him we are spiritually bankrupted; living in an oasis of what I would like to term as a spiritual famine.

My season of doubt and confusion occurred around the eighth month of pregnancy with my second child and a period of time when I was operating from a place of emptiness. During this time period my ex-husband and I were having some challenges in our marriage. Most of our problems stemmed from his many disappearing acts in conjunction with our finances. As issues intensified in the marriage we both agreed to separate for at least a year in order to work through our problems. Although, the thought of separating from my ex-husband for a year was the last thing I wanted to do it was necessary because I didn't want to bring another child into a hostile and stressful environment. Therefore, around June of 2000, I packed up most of my belongings and my ex-husband took me and my oldest son back to my hometown in Florida.

Shortly after my arrival in Florida, I landed a job and immediately began to work for about a month before the birth of our son. It truly was a blessing to gain employment as quick as I did while being eight months pregnant but I could not escape the fact that I was married but living like a single parent. As time passed I became more appreciative of the fact that I was gainfully employed and living in a stress free household but I still felt like a failure because my marriage resulted into separation. I tried my best to maintain a positive attitude and outlook on life because I did not want my children to sense any of my sadness. I spent several months walking around with a smile on my face as if everything was alright but I was dying inside. No one knew what I was feeling or thinking.

Until one day I decided to speak to the wife of my pastor at the time. Without going into detail this was a mistake on my part. Because of my mistake in judgment I paid for it dearly with the betrayal of someone who I thought I could trust to share confidential information with. A short time after this incident I stopped attending church because I lost all hope and confidence in those we suppose to seek spiritual guidance from, our spiritual leaders.

Consequently, matters within my marriage did not improve either. With the passing of time: days turned into months, and months turned into years. It seemed as if all the hopes and dreams my ex-husband and I had talked about prior to our marriage were slowly dissipating and there was nothing I could do about it. There were times when my ex-husband would occasionally visit me and our sons but each time there was a noticeable distance between the two of us. On two separate occasions we attempted to rekindle our marriage with a trip to the Bahamas but to no avail. Another reconciliation attempt occurred when my ex-husband relocated to Florida to be with the children and me.

For a brief period, happiness filled our marriage, it seemed like everything was going to be okay and we were going to make it as a family, but I was wrong. Less than six months after moving to Florida to be with us, my ex-husband decided to return to Georgia for a better paying job and that would be the last time we would be together as a family. Needless to say, nearly two months from the time my ex-husband left the children and me, I discovered that I was pregnant again.

Again, I put forth a good front and pretended as if nothing was wrong with our marriage or me. My acting would soon consume me to a devastating end because a few months later after finding out we were pregnant, I miscarried. Regardless of the fact, that there were continuous issues eroding our marriage, my ex-husband did make an effort to come to Florida to check on me. It was comforting to know during this traumatic time that he still had some feelings for me and I believe that's why he came to check on my well-being.

Besides not being totally over the betrayal I felt from trusting my formal pastor and his wife, the issues within my marriage and now dealing with a miscarriage, I fell into a deep depression after my ex-husband's visit. It would seem that only those persons who have lived through a miscarriage would understand the grief and sorrow I was experiencing. There were moments when I felt crazy and there were other times when I would blame myself. Occasionally, I would think to myself what could I have done differently that would have allowed me to carry my baby to full-term. Another thought would come across my mind: *Was there something I did where I deserved to loss my baby?* I would soon find out that it was best that I lost my child because several months after the miscarriage, my ex-husband came to visit again only to inform me that he had a girlfriend and that he wanted a divorce.

Hearing the word *divorce* coming out of his mouth was a bitter pill to swallow and it put me in a place of total despair, to the point I contemplated suicide shortly thereafter. This suicide attempt came around the time my children and I along with my mother were visiting relatives in Georgia for the Christmas holiday. As I reflect on that period of time in my life there was a tormenting spirit that was hovering over me and it wanted to take me out of this world.

Nevertheless, before I could go through with the decision to take my life, God sent an angel to whisper into my ear to let me know that everything concerning me and my children was going to be alright if I would just yield and trust him. Just like it is stated in Matthew 11:28 (NLT), *"come to me, all you who are weary and carry heavy burdens, and I will give you rest."* Hence, I yielded to the angelic host that was ministering to me at the time and began to rest in the arms of Jesus. I am so grateful and thankful that God had a way of escape mapped out for me because it would have been very selfish of me to know that I would have left my children motherless. It was also foolish of me to make a permanent decision to a temporary situation. I failed to realize during that time of my life that there was hope for tomorrow and that there is life after divorce.

Once, I regained my sanity, my visit with my family went on without a hitch and until this day no one has ever known that I attempted to take my life. Upon my return to Florida, I made a personal declaration that I was going to fight for my family but to my dismay God had other plans in store for me. God's plans included: (1) returning me back to my first love and that was Him; (2) restoring a relationship with his church; (3) to heal my heart and mind; and (4) to teach me the fundamentals of forgiveness.

On my road to restoration God spoke to me and said that he was like a consuming fire and he is a jealous God and that I should never put man or anything else before him (Deuteronomy 4:24; Exodus 34:14, *NIV*). I had to learn to re-divert the love I once had for my ex-husband back to God. I found out that the greatest mistake any person can make is to love someone so much that they lose themselves, their self-respect and confidence for the sake of love. Most of all, I found out that when we don't prioritize our relationships with God being first in line, those relationships will never succeed. I believe my failure to keep God first and foremost in my life was one of the reasons as to why my marriage didn't last in conjunction with other issues that plagued it. Now that I understand the importance of having God first in my life, I will never allow anything or anyone to take his place.

In addition, to God telling me to keep him number one in my life, he reminded me that I should never let what man do to me or to speak in their flesh hinder me from assembling with other believers. As it is stated in scripture: *"Let us not give up meeting together, as some are in the habit of doing, but let us encourage one another—and all the more as you see the Day approaching"* (Hebrews 10:25, NIV). I find it to be true that we should never attend church because of man but we should attend as part of our covenant relationship with God and his son Jesus Christ, not only to receive encouragement from the preached word of God to help us make it through everyday life but also to be an encouragement to other believers.

Healing the matters of my heart and mind was another important aspect to restoring my relationship with God. The process was a long and rigorous journey but necessary. Throughout the process of God healing my heart and mind he showed me the errors of my ways and told me that I no longer had time to focus on the hurtful things that had been said or done to me. Gaining this revelation opened up my eyes of understanding and I finally realized that I had spent too much time in life giving others control over the drawstrings of my heart and emotions. At one point in time, I allowed the actions of others to dictate how I was treated and how I responded. Hence, finding out that I no longer had to succumb to the negative treatment of others placed me on the final stage of restoration, the path of forgiveness.

Learning the fundamentals of forgiveness was a crucial part to restoring my relationship with Jesus Christ and my spiritual walk. Forgiveness is such a difficult thing to do because sometimes we will have to admit that we may have played a role in the wrong that was done. There are other times the wrong is done to us and we don't feel the need to forgive the person who did it to us. The act of forgiveness is also challenging because those we seek forgiveness from or must forgive; often do not remember the terrible misdeed that we are referring to. Additionally, there is a slight chance that when you approach that person and apologize to them for the wrong you did to them and ask them to forgive you, your wish may not be granted. However, do not be discouraged because the ownership of forgiveness is no longer yours it now rest on the shoulders of your offender or the person you sought forgiveness from.

Apart from the fact that most people may not remember what you are asking forgiveness for or what you are forgiving them of; forgiveness is not for the person who offended you but it is for you. We are instructed in scripture to *"...forgive others, and [we] will be forgiven"* (Luke 6:37 NLT). Thusly, forgiving others releases us from the bondages of anger and resentment and gives us a chance at living a loving, peaceful and joyful life.

Once, I understood that forgiving others was for me and not for the person who offended me; God told me to confront those persons who I believed had offended me as well as those persons who I had offended. The word of the Lord in Matthew 18:15 (NKJV) states that, *"If your brother sins against you, go and show him his fault, just between the two of you. If he listens to you, you have won your brother over."* Before I approached any of the people who I believed had offended me, I would pray to God and ask him to give me the right words to speak. Each time I prayed for guidance in my speech God would gave me such a boldness to speak the truth out of love in order to let the person know how their actions insulted me.

Two of the people who I approached to offer forgiveness for past transgressions had no clue as to what I was talking about. In spite of the fact that these individuals did not remember any of the offenses, I informed them what they had done to me. They reluctantly took ownership of the offenses and apologized, stating that if I had not come to them with my complaint they would have never known that they had offended anyone. From me approaching those individuals with my complaint of offense, they vowed to enhance their counseling skills and how they handled confidential information.

Regardless of the fact that my ex-husband and I were separated and he informed me that he no longer wanted to be married to me; I sought forgiveness for the manner in which I spoke to him and the way I treated him prior to our initial separation. To this date, I don't believe I ever heard the words "*I am sorry,*" spoken out of his mouth to me for what he had done to me but it doesn't matter anymore because I was liberated the very moment I acknowledged my wrongdoing. At the same time of apologizing for the things I did in our marriage, I took the opportunity to forgive him for all the things he had done to me throughout the duration of our marriage.

Even though I had to come to grips with some painful occurrences in my life, I found out later it was all part of God's plan to putting me on a journey of spiritual rejuvenation that would transform everything about me. This spiritual journey allowed me to be set free from all of my past hurts and pains. Most importantly, the spiritual journey of restoration granted me the opportunity to renew my personal relationship with God, a journey of spiritual restoration that was worth all of the hurt and pain!

CHAPTER FOUR

Spiritual Transformation

"Create in me a pure heart, O God and renew a
steadfast spirit within me"
Psalm 51:10 (NLT)

The greatest spiritual awakening a person can ever experience after they have been separated from God and his son Jesus Christ for a period of time or has become a new convert in the kingdom is to be transformed in their mind and spirit. My moment of spiritual awakening occurred the day I recommitted my life to God and prayed for him to reveal to me every ugly and detestable part of my being that would cause him to spur me out of his mouth. Petitioning God to grant such a request of this magnitude was not an easy thing to do because I did not know exactly what he would reveal to me. On the contrary, I thought to myself if I was going to live the rest of my life strictly for God then I had to accept whatever he showed me no matter how painful or repulsive it might be.

Therefore, God through his son Jesus Christ allowed me to see that I was quick tempered, impatient and at times hard to get along with. From this revelation, I was lead to pray to be given the fruit of God's spirit which consist of: patience, faithfulness, peace, joy, self-control, gentleness, goodness, love and kindness (Galatians 5:22-23). *Warning to the reader:* Be careful of what you ask God for because the tests you will face will be challenging and not for the meek at heart.

As soon as I asked God for the fruit of his spirit I was immediately tested in the area of patience. Patience is one of those character traits that I can honestly say I did not possess. As far back as I can remember and prior to my father's death, I was accustomed to getting what I wanted and when I wanted it.

However, later on in life I would discover that this is not true when it comes to God. He will not give you what you want just because you want it. For example, after working about two years at the job I had landed when I relocated to Florida after my separation from my then ex-husband; I wanted to transition into a new line of employment closely related to what I had received my graduate degree in. Each year, I would write my letter of resignation with the intent of submitting it to management but every time I would get up the nerve to turn it in God would tell me *now is not the time*. I got to a point that I became frustrated because I wanted so bad to move into something different. It took me an additional year and a half to figure out that things in life do not happen according to our timetable but on God's timetable.

Slowly, I began to understand what God was doing in my life. In fact, he was teaching me that not everything I wanted or desired would come immediately it would come at a time when I was mature enough and capable of handling the promotion. I am pleased to say that I was promoted in the form of another job that paid more than I was making at the previous job and it was in the field of my interest. Based on this experience, I can tell you that God will allow you to stay where you are no matter how long it

Spiritual Transformation

takes for you to learn the lesson or lessons that he has for you to learn. The best advice that I could ever give to anyone who is going through a life experience at this very moment would be to look for opportunities within your predicament to learn and grow from, so that you may move onto the next lesson that awaits you.

Once it was evident that I understood the importance of patience and the value of waiting on the Lord to move on my behalf, the next fruit of the spirit that I had to master was the fruit of faithfulness. Faithfulness, in this instance, dealt with tithes and offerings. I must be truthful and honest that the test of faithfulness in tithes and offering was difficult for me to learn because I had to be reconditioned in my mindset in regards to giving.

For years I had been exposed to the wrong thought process about giving to the church. I had been conditioned to believe that you pay your bills first and then give whatever was left over toward your tithes and offering. There were many critics during those times in my life that believed that the money you gave to the church went to the pastor and provided for his luxuries in life. Until God began to deal with me in the area of giving; I never knew that I was operating in disobedience. I soon found out the importance of tithing and sowing seed offerings. I learned my giving was not for the benefit of God because everything I own belongs to him anyway, he wanted to see if my allegiance was with him. Simply stated, God wanted to see what I treasured the most, Him or money.

In the midst of God teaching me about faithfulness, he also was grooming me in the areas of peace and joy. By this point in time in my life I was contending with a major lawsuit against me by a well-known financial institution. Although, I was dealing with an abundance of stressful issues, I soon found out why our

Lord and Savior had me on this journey. God was trying to get me to understand that I needed to learn how to remain at peace no matter what my circumstances were and to trust him to fight my battles. Several months after dealing with the lawsuit, it was finally settled and in my favor. I must say that everything that I had to endure was worth all the sleepless nights and the many tears I cried because not only did I learn the real reason behind tithing and sowing seed offerings.

Furthermore, I learned a valuable lesson that we should never allow negative situations to rob us of our peace or joy. I had to learn that my peace was not based on everything going right in my life but it comes from the peace of God that dwells within me. For the word of the Lord says that *"his peace will guard* [our] *hearts and minds, as* [we] *live in Christ Jesus"* (Philippians 4:7b, NLT). The same holds true for joy. In Nehemiah 8:10b *(NIV)*, it is written that we should *"not grieve, for the joy of the Lord is our strength."* In accordance to this scripture, I decided since God would fight my battles for me than I would live a joyful life no matter what.

The next fruit of the Spirit that I was thrust into learning was self-control and gentleness. As it was mentioned earlier that God had revealed to me that I had a bad temperament and trouble controlling my mouth. I had the worst character flaw when it came to dealing with people; I was short tempered, easily irritated and could go from zero to a hundred in a second.

There were times when people would say things to me and I would respond in an aggressive and mean way. As you can see I seriously needed help with controlling my emotions. I needed to learn how to respond to people in a more compassionate and gentle manner; and with me acknowledging this fact, I was tested on countless accounts.

Spiritual Transformation

For example, there was an incident that occurred at one of my previous places of employment when a parent got very combative with me and literally wanted to fight me in front of their children but being that the Lord was working on me, he directed me through the Holy Spirit to hold my peace and not say a word. If truth be told, I *really, really, really, really, really* wanted to say something back to that parent but I knew that if I didn't remain calm and maintain a peaceful and pleasant disposition then the next test concerning self-control and the treatment toward an irate person would be harder and much longer.

According to scripture found in Proverbs 13:3 *(NLT)," those who control their tongue will have a long life; opening your mouth can ruin everything."* Hence, I let the parent have her say while at the same time I keep uttering *"Peace be still"* silently in my spirit. Shortly thereafter, I came to the conclusion based on this incident that I must function from a place of wisdom and kindness in responding to someone. I also came into the realization that there will be times when I will need to take the high road and know that I don't have to be right all the time in every situation.

Subsequently, I found out later that the rationale for the parent's hostility toward me stemmed from the fact that she and her husband was having problems in their marriage and that they were facing an eviction from their home. I concluded from this encounter, that people (including myself) sometimes don't know how to properly convey their cry for help.

Kindness and goodness were the next elements of God's characteristics that were on my schedule of training. The spirit of kindness and goodness are fruits that are interchangeable. It is impossible for a person to be kind to another person without them being good to them at the same time. Geoffrey Nunberg, describes kindness "as the quality or state of being kind"[1]. If you think about it, kindness is equivalent to that of grace. In the same likeness, goodness can be viewed as mercy. As part of my development in gaining the spirit of kindness and goodness, God had me to give out of my abundance to those I passed along the way throughout my daily travels. My giving did not always encompass monetarily gifts. Sometimes, I was instructed to give a word of encouragement.

At other times, I was told to give a smile or extend a hug to someone who seemed to be going through something in life. In the course of obtaining the spirit of kindness and goodness, I had an epiphany that I must give the same level of kindness and goodness to others as it was afforded to me by Jesus Christ. The extension of kindness and goodness is not a one-time occurrence but it extends over the course of a lifetime. According to Titus 3:4-5a (NLT),"*when God our Savior revealed his kindness and love, he saved us, not because of the righteous things we had done, but because of his mercy.*"

The final stage of the development of the fruit of the spirit was love. During a conversation one day with my spiritual mother, we begin to discuss the topic about gaining the fruit of God's spirit. She so happened to mention to me that once you obtain the spirit of love then you have gained all of the other fruits of the spirit.

Although, I gained the fruit of the spirit differently from what my spiritual mother had stated to me, I learned them the way God wanted me to learn them. Even so, I do agree with my spiritual mother that love is a key factor to obtaining the fruits of God's spirit. At some point in the phase of achieving the spirit of love, the Holy Spirit brought to my attention another character flaw that needed correction and that was being critical of others. The

Lord told me that I could no longer be judgmental of others but I had to love them where they were in life and to remain supportive of them as they made their way back to wholeness and discovering who God created them to be and do on earth. Love is that four letter action word that has to be performed more than said. On several occasions, I was challenged to love those who I knew would not reciprocate the same love back to me. In the face of not receiving the same kind of love that I projected on others, the word of the Lord commands us to love one other in the same way he loved us (John 15:12, *NIV*).

There is no way in the world that I can claim to be a child of God and profess to love him and his son, Jesus Christ and not be able love those around me. In other words, I must show forth the same agape love that God has and continues to shower me with each and every passing day. I am grateful to God that he loves me so much that he went out of his way to ensure that I knew the significance of loving others.

The development of the fruit of God's spirit caused me to face some harsh realities about myself that I would have never confronted if I hadn't prayed the prayer for him to show me the areas of my life that displeased him. Developing the fruit of God's spirit forced me to take a good look in the mirror at myself and face the fact that there were defects in my personality and that I could no longer hide behind the façade of being that perfect person that I pretended to be. If there is one thing I can take away from this experience it would be that no one can ever approach me and tell me about the negative characteristics of my past behavior because God has shown them to me and gave me room to correct them.

Most importantly, God not only reconstructed the defective parts of my character but he did it so that he could maximize the spiritual gifts he placed in me and that I would be a better representative of his kingdom. Throughout the duration of my spiritual transformation I constantly spoke this statement to Jesus: *"Lord, I never want to say or do anything to your people that will mislead them or bring harm to them."*

Thusly, he kept me secretly hidden and continues to work on all the areas of my life to include: the way I think as well as my character traits. With that being said, I am still on the potter's wheel being transformed into the likeness of Jesus Christ.

CHAPTER FIVE

Point of Spiritual Growth

"Don't copy the behavior and customs of this world, but let God transform you into a new person by changing the way you think......"
Romans 12:2 (NLT)

Spiritual growth is a continuous progression in one's walk with Jesus and cannot be captured in an instant vacuum. Everything about a person changes throughout the spiritual growth phase. The person's entire outlook on life changes to include: how they view themselves, the world around them, how they act and react to certain situations or problems, and how they handle those problems when they arise. Normally, people who are transitioning and growing spiritually view themselves in a positive light. These individuals strive to remain optimistic about their near future, in spite of their circumstances being challenging and a bit bleak.

There are varying degrees to a person's spiritual growth. Growth for one person may not be the same for another person and vice-versa. As it relates to scripture, we are all at different levels in our faith with Christ Jesus (1John 2:12-14, *NLT*). Therefore, a point of spiritual growth for one person might occur when they realize that there are no more options left on the table for them to choose from and they no longer have the answer to their problem. Meanwhile, the complexities of life may bring another person to their knees when they realize that they can no longer do the same thing the same way and expect a different result. However, another person maybe standing at the crossroads of life and have come to the conclusion that they cannot live their life without having a personal relationship with Jesus Christ.

On the other hand, there is a group of people who realize that once their mode of thinking and their way of living has been transformed they can no longer participate in activities that once brought them pleasure and comfort. These same groups of people also understand that they cannot be surrounded by people, places or things that may compromise their spiritual growth. The realization of these points reflects on a person's spiritual maturity and how far they have come from the time they became a new convert in the kingdom of God.

My point of spiritual growth took place the moment I re-established my relationship with Jesus and vowed to live the remaining portion of my life for him. From this declaration, I realized that there was no turning back to my old self or ways of doing things; it was time to grow-up spiritually. Additionally, it was time for me to live the new life that I had received from recommitting my life to serving the Lord, and what better way of doing so then reading and meditating on his word.

As it was mentioned earlier in Chapter One, that as a young child I had limited exposure to the word of God and not too many people knew how to explain it to me when I had questions. For that very reason, I found it imperative for me to seek the word for myself as a means to find the answers to the questions I had about life. It is written in scripture: *"Study to show thyself approved unto*

God, a workman that needth not be ashamed, rightly dividing the word of truth" (2 Timothy 2:15, *KJV*).

Nevertheless, as I got more into the word of God my prayer life begin to develop and I found myself seeking Jesus for guidance and direction in my life. As stated in Proverbs 3:6, that we should seek the will of the Lord in all that we do, and he will show us the path we should take [paraphrased]. The development of a prayer life plays a vital role to the growth of a child of God and is essential on various accounts. Developing a prayer life also gives us direct access to God through Jesus Christ and it strengthens our faith. The development of a prayer life also gives us an opportunity to thank God for all he has done for us and it causes us to change the way we think about the troubling things that are happening in our life (Philippians 4:6, *NLT*).

Moreover, the development of a prayer life opens the door to our spirit where God can minister to the issues of our life as well as give us insight into our future. There are so many other things I could continue to speak on about the development of a prayer life but I will not at this point. There is one thing, however, I would like for you to take away from this discussion and that is as we get into a posture of prayer our praying will lead us into a mode of praise. In turn we create an atmosphere that is conducive for the Holy Spirit to appear in the midst of us worshipping Jesus Christ.

The depth of my spiritual growth extended beyond just reading and studying the word of God and praying. As part of God's spiritual growth plan for me during that season of my life, he afforded me countless opportunities to attend empowerment conferences that spoke on the issues that I was working through. Although, it was great that I was given the chance to attend such conferences; it was a bit challenging for me because I was being pushed out of my comfort zone; and I was not accustomed to that.

Oftentimes, it is difficult for a person to move out of their area of familiarity because of the fear of the unknown. However, moving forward to an unknown place can be beneficial and have surprising results. Hence, as a result of me being pushed out of my comfort zone it became easier for me to fellowship, develop friendships, and communicate with other believers and unbelievers. As I reflect back on those times in my life, I truly believe that as God moved me out of the land of familiarity he placed within me a spirit of boldness and tenacity to the point that I was not afraid of meeting new people. I have noticed that it is easier for me now to talk about God, His word and his son Jesus Christ with people I am in close relationship with as well as with total strangers.

In addition, to attending conferences I was lead to read inspirational materials and books that spoke on discovering the call and destiny of one's life. I also read books that were designed to spark the readers' intuitiveness and challenge them to stretch in their faith. It is, in my opinion, that reading the bible along with other inspirational literature adds to a person's spiritual growth and provides them with clarity as to why they were created and placed here on Earth.

Consequently, it came apparent to me that I had reached another pivotal point in my spiritual growth when the things that people would say to me no longer had an impact on me and I didn't find the need to respond to their comments. I believe this is the point in my spiritual journey where the Holy Spirit became more and more evident in my life. As it is stated in John 16:13, *"When the Spirit of truth comes, he will guide you into all truth...."*

Being led by the Holy Spirit in my everyday life became a pattern of living for me. I found out in my journey with Jesus that I could no longer rely on the carnality of my flesh to provide me with instruction on how I should act or react to others and certain situations.

I find it to be vitally important in the era in which we are living in, that we must remain sensitive to the Holy Spirit and allow him to be that beckon in our lives that guides us in every facet of our life. How amazing it would be if everyone operated in the Holy Spirit, especially in today's modern society when people say and do just about anything without taking into consideration the impact of the words they use to express themselves and how their actions may have adverse effects on others.

In conjunction to learning the importance of the Holy Spirit being present in my life, it became apparent that I had to operate in the spirit of humility on a consistent basis. I learned firsthand that there will be events and situations that will occur in one's life when we must set aside our pride and ask for help from someone; even if it's the person we said would be the last person on Earth that we go to for any assistance.

I knew the day that I had to swallow my pride and ask for help was a day I had grown again spiritually. I say this because it had not been easy for me to reach out to others for assistance due to lack of trust in people. I had to grasp the understanding that not everyone is out to cause me any harm and those who were willing to help me would not necessarily do so, just to throw it back into my face that they provided me with assistance. I had to come to the conclusion that God does use people as part of granting our prayer request of assistance. I must say that this was a valuable lesson well learned and it shall not be forgotten. Moreover, my ability to share with others of what I have endured in life and what God has seen me through marked another milestone of accomplishment in my spiritual growth. If truth be told, it is not always easy for someone to be transparent and share pertinent information about themselves with people they are not familiar with. There is a preconceived notion that sharing some of the intimate parts of our journey will result in guilt and shame and people in the end will not be receptive to our witnessing but that is far from the truth.

A testimony, in fact, could be proven to be beneficial not only for the person giving the testimony but for the person hearing the testament as well. The word of the Lord states *"that we overcome the enemy by the blood of the Lamb and the word of our testimony"* (Rev. 12:11a, NIV). In essence, the more we share with others what we have experienced in life; the more we become comfortable in telling our story and the stronger we are in our faith.

Finally, you know that you have reached another level in spiritual growth when you are able to move forward in faith despite your circumstances. For example, I had a life altering and near death experience in the summer of 2005. During this particular season in my life I was faced with some real life challenges: my employer had laid me off and I fell ill. The place where I was working abruptly closed its doors and I was out of a job. The organization that managed the business did not give any warning that the business was going under. On top of being out of work, I ended up being hospitalized and in a coma due to a bad tooth. Yes, you heard me right, a bad tooth! This happened because my dentist at the time attempted to savage a tooth that I believe was not worth saving and due to his unsolicited efforts, I incurred an infection that over time metastasized throughout my body.

In order for you to grasp a full understanding of the aforementioned scenario and how it lead to what I would like to describe as a point of spiritual growth, let me take you back to the time this event actually occurred. It all started on July 12, 2005, and on this particular summer evening I was preparing for bed, I had just taken my pain medication and antibiotics that had been prescribed for me because I had been dealing with a bad toothache and infection for about two months. After I had taken the medication I proceeded to my mother's room (with whom I was living with at the time) to tell her something but before I could open my mouth I fell across her bed foaming at the mouth. She told my oldest son to call 911 and all I can remember was telling him to go next door to get Sister White. Based on my mother's account, Mrs. White rushed over immediately and as she entered the room she made a bold statement: *"devil take your hands off this child, you can't have her because she belongs to God!"*

Throughout this entire episode my mother told me that before the paramedics could arrive I began to have convulsions. Shortly thereafter, the paramedics arrived and placed me on a gurney and transported me to the local hospital. Upon arrival at the hospital, the emergency room doctor asked my mother a series of questions such as: *What was my name? If I was under the influence of any drugs or alcohol; and did I suffer from depression or if I was seeking attention?* Her response to all these ridiculous questions was *"NO!"*

In accordance to my mother's memory, I stop breathing three times and after the third time she insisted that I be placed on a respirator. After this occurred my mother informed my sisters who were living in Georgia of my condition and they came home to check things out as well as help out with my children.

During my stay in the hospital there were various individuals who came to visit me and one person in particular was my cousin who is a minister. I was told that she and her prayer partner came to my hospital room to pray healing over my body but to her surprise the Holy Spirit took hold of me and allowed me to speak these words, *"This illness is not unto death."* When I was later informed of this, I could not belief it because before I went through this sickness I had asked the Lord to use me in a way that would glorify him and draw my family closer to him. I must say he did just what I asked of him and until this day I never found out the full extinct to my illness but I know God healed me from that infirmity. As I reflect on that time in my life God showed me as well as to others that he is a healer, he is the Great Physician, he is *Jehovah-rapha*.

A week after this incident occurred and I was discharged from the hospital I gained a sense in my spirit that my life would never be the same as it had been before. And I was right because not long after being home from the hospital, God instructed me to relocate back to the Atlanta area and I thought to myself, *"God you have to be joking."* The move would prove to be a major leap of faith for me because I had recently gotten out of the hospital, I had not fully recovered, and I would have nowhere to live and no prospect of employment. After receiving the instruction from God to move, I had to stop myself from looking at my circumstances in the natural realm and rely on my faith in Him. This is the moment I believe I had reached another point of spiritual growth; the ability to hear God, to listen to his instructions as well as to obey them without questioning him.

Based on everything I have shared with you thus far regarding my spiritual journey, I have gained some invaluable information about God and myself. I deduce that not everything in life has to be picturesque perfect in order to be obedient to the instructions of God. Once you have been transformed spiritually and placed on a path toward spiritual growth, you can never go back to your former self because it is impossible for you to take up residence in two dimensions of thought without the inheritance of conflict. For that reason, we all must strive daily to commit our lives to God and maintain our trust and belief in his son Jesus Christ as he continues to transform our way of thinking and living.

CHAPTER SIX

Building of Relentless Faith

*"For you know that when your faith
is tested, your endurance has a chance to grow"*
James 1:3 (NIV)

The building of relentless faith adheres to a continuous and arduous process, consisting of a variety of tests and trials throughout an individuals' lifetime. Tests and trials act as a catalyst to a person's spiritual growth and development. Tests and trials can be viewed as challenges that keep a person inclined to constantly seeking God and praying for his guidance for their everyday life, so that they do not become stagnant or complacent in their faith walk.

When we face the same assortment of challenges or obstacles in life, we often mischaracterize it as a ploy sent by the enemy to derail us from the plans and purpose that God has preordained for us to accomplish in life; however, that is not always the case. Many times God allows certain things to happen in our life as a means to maintain our attention and serve as a pruning mechanism, in order to get rid of those things that are useless and nonessential to the calling or destiny that is on our life. It is my assumption that God prunes us not because we have done something wrong and we need correction, but he does it because he loves us so much that he wants the very best for us and desires for us to be fruitful or should I say be productive spiritually.

There were times when I passed the test that was thrust upon me and there were other times when I had to retake the test again. Taking spiritual tests are similar to those tests that we take while in school; the only difference between the two is that the test you take in school you may only get one chance to retake. When it comes to spiritual tests, you will be required to take them as many times as needed until you get it right or you have learned the intended lesson or lessons. There are other times when some tests will reoccur because God wants to make sure you are well-equipped and prepared to handle the next dimension of elevation that you will step into.

On the other hand, some tests occur in our life because God wants to know whether our faith lies within what we own, in ourselves or in Him. Whatever the case maybe, when you are confronted with tests of many kinds, the word of God in James 1:12 (NLT) states that: *"God blesses those who patiently endure testing and temptation. Afterward they will receive the crown of life that God has promised to those who love him."*

A prime example of the testing of faith can be found in the lives of the three Hebrew boys: Shadrach, Meshach and Abednego (Daniel 3:13-25, NIV). These three young men were thrown into a fiery furnace by a ruler by the name of king Nebuchadnezzar because they refused to bow down and worship his idol god (a golden statute). Shadrach, Meshach, and Abednego exhibited the epitome of faith during their season of testing. These three young men had so much faith in Jesus that they were not even moved or upset over the fact they were about to be burned alive. They made this statement to king Nebuchadnezzar in Daniel 3:17-18 exclaiming their faithfulness to God,

If we are thrown in the blazing furnace, the God whom we serve is able to save us. He will make it clear to you, Your Majesty. But even if he doesn't, we want to make it clear to you, Your Majesty that we will never serve your gods or worship the gold statute you have set up.

In the face of a threat by a cruel and oppressive ruler who wanted Shadrach, Meshach and Abednego to do something against their belief system, these three young men were adamant in their belief in God and were not deterred from trusting that he would provide a way of escape for them. This story shows us that the resilience and determination of an individual or even a group of people cannot be crushed or trampled on because of external forces. Based on the bravery of Shadrach, Meshach and Abednego, we can deduce that God will provide protection and comfort in the time of adversity and at the end of a trying storm he will be glorified.

Despite the fact that I have seen the many changes that God has taken me through in my spiritual walk with Him and his son Jesus Christ, I have noticed on more than a few occasions that he placed me in the refiners' fire as a way to get rid of the lingering qualities or characteristics that did not resemble him; and that would otherwise hinder my spiritual growth. From the very first time I asked God to give me the fruit of his spirit, I have been tested over and over again in the areas of: love, patience (long-suffering), self-control, peace, joy, faithfulness, goodness, gentleness and kindness.

Although, love was one of the last fruits that I acquired; it has been the first one that I have been tested on a continuous basis.

There have been several occurrences where God has used family members and perfect strangers to test me in this area, to see if I would extend agape love to them as he has extended toward me. I posit that as Christians we are frequently given a love check up by God because he wants to see what's in our heart and if we are abiding by the commandment given to us by Jesus Christ in John 15:17 to *"love each other."* A love check-up is needed now more than ever because of the society in which we are currently living in and the climate of unrest in many communities across America and the world at-large. The love check I am referring to is the ability to love others who would otherwise hate you. I know that there may be some who would disagree and that's okay but one thing we must all remember is that Jesus will return one day soon and we should want to be right in his sight.

Besides love being the number one ranking character trait for Christendom and the quality that we are most often tested on, you and I will be confronted by a multitude of remedial test taking on the remaining fruits of the spirit: patience, self-control, peace, joy, faithfulness, goodness, gentleness and kindness. These particular qualities keep us grounded and focused on Christ, how we should live our lives and maintain our sanity in a world full of chaos.

Even though, it is not always easy to pass retakes in the area of self-control and being peaceful and faithful and showing forth joy, goodness, gentleness and kindness in times of trouble and hardship in one's life; it is necessary because the world has run out of what it considers to be genuine answers to everyday problems. People of the world are now searching any and everywhere for answers to their problems. What better way to give them the answer then by showing them that we the children of light know how to have control over our emotions and can be steadfast and immovable in our faith in Jesus Christ (1Corinthians 15:58, *NLT*).

Here's a summation of some of the ways in which the assistance of the Holy Spirit has helped me to be able to establish a sound and relentless faith in God as well as make it through difficult times of tests and trials: (1.) praying for wisdom, (2.) operating from a spirit of discernment, (3.) invoking of the Holy Spirit, (4.) learning how to put on the full armor of God, (5.) meditating on the word of God on a regular basis, (6.) seeking wise counsel, and (7.) maintaining a teachable spirit.

1. Pray for Wisdom

In an age when many people in today's society make decisions abruptly based on ill-gotten information and how they feel in the flesh, it is crucial that those of us who believe in Jesus Christ pray for wisdom before we make any major decision concerning our personal and professional lives as well as prior to responding to any comments directed toward us by others.

Based on Ephesians 1:17 it is stated that: *"asking God, the glorious Father of our Lord Jesus Christ, to give you spiritual wisdom and insight so that you might grow in your knowledge of God."* Praying for wisdom inherently grants us the opportunity to find out what God desires for us to do in life in accordance to his principles and statues. Praying for wisdom provides us with good sound judgment regarding the paths that we should take in life and at the same time gives us an indication of the foolish choices and paths we should avoid altogether.

Additionally, wisdom allows us to distinguish between right and wrong and opens us up to the eagerness to learn new things.[2]

To a certain extent wisdom is similar to that of knowledge. Knowledge exposes us to new information, whereas, wisdom tells us what to do with that new information we have gained. Solomon said it best in Proverbs 3:18, *"wisdom is a tree of life to those who embrace her, happy are those who hold her tightly."* Based on this assertion, it is wise to say that in order for a person to live out a fruitful life they must not only pray on a continuous basis for wisdom but once it is obtained they must utilize it every day.

2. Operate from a Spirit of Discernment

Operating from a spirit of discernment and praying for God to infuse you with wisdom are similar in nature. Operating from a spirit of discernment and possessing wisdom are essential to a person who is attempting to live a life for Jesus Christ and making it through life's challenges. They both provide you with the intuitiveness to know the difference between right and wrong; and how to make appropriate choices that will keep you out of trouble based on previous experience.

Furthermore, our ability to operate in a mode of discernment for the most part affords us the opportunity to sense in the spirit realm when things are not right in our immediate surroundings; what the true intentions are of those we are in relationship with and gives us the option to make rational decisions of whether or not we should remain in those relationships, if we desire to do so. Moreover, operating from a spirit of discernment serves as a guiding force in our life; the choices we should make in accordance to the will of God and how we should apply the wisdom we have gained throughout the testing of our faith. For the word of the Lord says in Proverbs 5:2," *you will show discernment and your lips will express what you've learned."*

3. Remain Sensitive to the Holy Spirit

As a part of building a relentless faith, it is important to remain sensitive to the Holy Spirit. Remaining sensitive to the Holy Spirit provides us with an advocate with God our Father, especially at times when we know we should pray but simply do not know what to pray for. Remaining sensitive to the Holy Spirit also provides us with the insight whereby he brings back into our remembrance of the things that we previously learned as well as the things that God has spoken to us that he would do for us. As it is stated in John 14:26 *NLT*, *"But when the Father sends the Advocate as my representative-the Holy Spirit-will teach you everything and will remind everything I have told you."* It is important to mention that the Holy Spirit not only serves in the capacity of an advocate but stands in place of Jesus Christ as our comforter until he returns.

Subsequently, the Holy Spirit poses as our inner compass; guiding us in our speech, thoughts and the path we should take in life. Just like that of operating from a place of discernment, the Holy Spirit provides us with the wisdom on how we should live out our lives. As a result to remaining sensitive to the Holy Spirit, I have been afforded the opportunity to receive heavenly downloads regarding strategic plans and creative ideas on how to confront and handle certain issues that arose in my life.

4. Clothe yourself with the Full Armor of God

In conjunction to having the word of God stored up in your spirit, it is important to be properly clothed with the full armor of God as a means to build relentless faith and maintain momentum in times of testing. The armor of God serves as kryptonite to the enemy for it weakens his blows, to the point his ability to discourage you and any attempt to grab hold of you is lessened. In order to combat the enemy's hits, you will need to know what the armor consist of and where each piece of garment must to be placed figuratively on your body. As a means to provide clarity, the armor of God includes: the belt of truth, the breastplate of righteousness, the shoes of peace that comes from the Good News, the shield of faith, the helmet of salvation, and the sword of the Spirit which represents the word of God (Ephesians 6:14-18). Each piece of garment is specifically earmarked to combat any plot or scheme targeted at you by the enemy.

First, the belt of truth, gives you the ability to distinguish between the truth of God and the lies of the enemy. Being that the enemy is the author of lies, this garment is especially needed. Secondly, there is the breastplate of righteousness and its purpose is to guard our hearts against the betrayal of others. The heart is protected in this manner because the heart is the core to our emotions, what we value the most in life and how we view ourselves.

Thirdly, there are the shoes of peace, which is representative of the Good News of Jesus Christ. The shoes of peace are necessary because they provide us with the fortitude to stand and spread the message of truth even when people are not receptive to it. Next, there is the shield of faith which blocks the fiery darts shot at us by the enemy. The fiery darts that I am referring to that the shield of faith protects us against involves: temptations, obstacles of many kinds, and false accusations. The shield of faith also guards us against the disbelief that we are not victorious in Christ Jesus.

Then, there is the helmet of salvation, which protects our minds against the enemy from infusing doubt into our thoughts; that we are not afforded the opportunity to receive salvation from God and his son Jesus Christ. Lastly, there is the sword of the

Spirit which is representative of the word of God. All of the other garments of God were armors of defense but the sword of the Spirit is the only offensive mechanism of the armors used to undergird us with the truth of God's word, so that we may trust and believe him more and not the lies employed by the prince of darkness.

5. Daily Meditation of Scripture

It is important for every person who is striving to build a relentless faith to put forth the effort to meditate on scripture on a daily basis, whether or not they are dealing with issues in their life. We are instructed in scripture to meditate on the word of God day and night of each day (Joshua 1:8). This instruction is only beneficial to the person who strives daily to know and understand the word and how it can assist them in making it through life. Throughout my journey in dealing with problematic issues in life, I have learned that by memorizing one verse a day pertaining to a particular issue is helpful. In doing so, I have been able to maintain my confidence in Jesus Christ regularly so that when trouble does appear in my life I am equipped with a word to speak to my circumstance and combat any negative thoughts that would suggest that God cannot solve my problem.

6. Seek Wise Counsel

It has always been part of my conviction that prior to making a decision no matter how big or small that decision may have been concerning my life, to first seek out God for direction and then follow-up with guidance from someone who I thought I could trust and believe would provide me with good sound advice based on their knowledge of God and his word. In accordance to Proverbs 12:15, *"fools think their own way is right but the wise listen to others."* Besides seeking God regarding matters in my life, I was fortunate enough to have a spiritual mother who had a special relationship with God like that of Elijah, who was able to minister to me in a profound and personable way. Although, my relationship with my spiritual mother is not as it was when I began my spiritual journey into a life of wholeness, her guidance to me during a treacherous point in my life, her wisdom and friendship has meant so much to me and she will forever hold a special place in my heart. Because of her unselfishness and motherly mantle, I am now able to do the same for others based on my own personal experiences in life and the relationship I have with God.

Thusly, when situations call for them, we should always seek godly counselor as well as provide wise counselor to others if it becomes necessary. Moreover, if you are a person who is currently dealing with a problem in your life I would suggest that you look to God for instructions and pray that he will place the right person in your path that will provide you with godly advice and spiritually guide you to the place where you will discover the answers pertaining to your particular situation.

7. Maintain a Teachable Spirit

The final stage I belief has been beneficial to me making it through seasons of testing and multiple types of trials as well as the building blocks of a strong faith in the Lord has been the capacity of maintaining an open and teachable spirit. In view of the fact, that spiritual growth can be considered an essential component to our faith walk with Jesus Christ; it is vitally important for us to keep ourselves open to learning new things because it provides us with the room to gain more fundamental principles for Christian living and witnessing for our personal lives in general and the treatment of others.

There are some people who reach a prominent level in life and assume that because of their status in life they have no more room for growth. On the other hand, there are some people who can only be taught life lessons through experiencing tests and trials. For instance, a parent warning their teenager or adult child about being careful and watchful of the type of people they associate with. Some children will heed the warning of their parents, while others will ignore their parent's teaching and end up in trouble. Meanwhile, there is a small group of people who are so intrigued with learning new and exciting things about life they adhere to corrective criticism and make every effort in becoming better people.

Nevertheless, no matter what status a person holds in their life and how successful they might become based on man's standard, they are never too young or too old to learn something new whether it is about themselves, others or even a new approach to solving problems. In connection to this train of thought there is an old saying: *The day you stop learning is the day you are no longer living.* Likewise, Proverbs 23:12 states that we should *"commit [ourselves]to instruction; [and] listen carefully to words of knowledge."* For this reason, we should strive each and every day to learn something from others as well as share with others what we have learned in life.

Overall, the intent of every test and trial that we all will experience at one point in time in our life do not necessarily occur as means to cause us any harm or danger but to shape our character, to equip us with a powerful testimony in order to be effective witnesses for the kingdom, to further propel us into destiny, and to glorify God. As a testament to the building of relentless faith in my life, transpired the day I made this personal declaration to myself:

Giving up is not an option nor is it part of my vocabulary. I will press through any and every test and trial that may come my way; with or without support from family or friends to provide encouragement to me. No matter what, I will keep moving forward until I see the promises of God manifest in my life.

Ultimately, the key factor that sustains us during cycles of tests and trials is our ability with the help of the Holy Spirit to maintain a resilient and perseverant spirit, the reassurance of the word of God, the faith and trust we have in the God we serve and the countless times that Jesus has proven himself to be trustworthy and dependable in our life.

CHAPTER SEVEN

Destiny Realized

*"...God has revealed the meaning
of the dreams to you...."*
Genesis 41:39(NLT)

It takes some people a lifetime to reach the pinnacles of achievement and come into the fullest of their calling. Most of the time people spend the majority of their lives being a square peg in a round world, allowing others to dictate to them what they perceive to be the best choice for them or simply push them into a place they were not created to reign over or destined to uphold. These same people never come into the fulfillment of their destiny. At one point in time I use to be one of those individuals who did not know what I was created and preordained to do here on Earth and I allowed others to tell me what they thought was best for my life. During the early stages of my adult years I spent most of the time making some life and career choices that I now believe had nothing to do with the plans and purpose that God had placed on my life.

Since that time I have discovered that the only way I was going to find out what God had destined for me to accomplish in life was to venture out into the unknown, without any indication as to where he was taken me. I knew I had to be confident that I was following God's cues based on his instructions and to trust and believe that I had truly heard from Him. One the biggest leaps of faith I have taken in life was to give up my employment with a school system that I had been employed with for over seven years in order to pursue my doctoral degree. Many people in my life and inner circle did not understand what I was doing at the time and I believe some of them are still reluctant to this date regarding the decision I made for my life.

Overall, there will be a time in everyone's life when we must move forward in boldness and faith, even when we don't quite understand nor have a clue as to where we are headed. When we have a sense within our spirit that the Lord has spoken to us regarding our decision to move forward in faith, we you cannot concern ourselves with the opinions of naysayers because only God knows where he's taking us in life. With that being said, there will come a time in your life when you too must take a leap of faith in order to discover what God has ordained for you to accomplish here on Earth and you must never allow the fear of the unknown to sabotage your destiny or denounce your rightful place in the kingdom. It is noteworthy to mention, that the day you come into the realization of the destiny that is on your life is the day that you truly begin to live.

It is without question that we all have a destiny on our lives and we have the propensity to reach the highest of heights of that calling in record timing and instantaneously. But first we must be willing to trust God and ourselves with the choices that we make pertaining to our life. Based on this assertion and all of the things that God has seen me through over the years from a lack of identity, loneliness and not knowing where I belonged in the world to periods of isolation and starving for love and affection; I have come to the conclusion that the more I let go of my will for God's will, the more I discover the things he has created me to do for his kingdom.

Furthermore, I have discovered that the more I let go of who I thought I was and wanted to be and grasp hold to God; that is when I began to be what he called and made me to be. I am discovering each and every day that God blesses me with breathe to breath that I am free to be me, free to be the best me he created me to be and free to dream big dreams that surpasses all understanding and to live to see those dreams come into fruition. In the same likeliness, God requires that you become the best you that you can possibility transform into and that can only be accomplished by you truly knowing who he called you to be in comparison to what you were not created to be or what people think you should be.

As part of the bigger picture of the destiny and calling that God has placed on my life, I have been given a charge in conjunction to the path that he has allowed me to travel to inspire others on how to move out of a life of obscurity and mediocrity into a life filled with an abundance of possibilities. Also, to inform every person who may be living a down-trodden and defeated life that they no longer have to live a substandard life or a life that is beneath their privilege. In retrospect, I believe I have been destined to inform these same individuals that as a part of their divine destiny they have a right to live a life that is prosperous and full of purpose.

Moreover, I have been called to be an agent of change someone who will impact the culture of mankind. As an agent of change, I have been charged with the responsibility, as all Christians have been given the charge, to model the character and mindset of Jesus Christ. We are encouraged by the illustration given to us in 1 Corinthians 4:16 by the Apostle Paul, that we should emulate the same demeanor he displayed during his quest to spread the Good News of Jesus Christ. The testament of Paul should encourage every believer in the kingdom of God to strive to imitate the behavior that is above reproach and a life that is pleasing unto God.

Overall, the greatest lasting impact that we could make as a people in an era that is filled with uncertainty, agnosticism, and high levels of phobias on every level; would be to come into the knowledge of our calling and go forth in truth in our respective occupations and communities and provide substantive solutions to problems that affect a select group of people.

Nonetheless, based on all the things I have described so far I believe are part of my destiny and calling. I feel that God has also instructed me to tell others everywhere he sends me that they have the right to be happy and be granted the desires of their heart. As it is stated in the word of the Lord in Psalm 37:4 *(NLT)*, *"take delight in the Lord and he will give you your heart's desires."*

As I continue to follow Jesus Christ, I am forever amazed by how much creativeness and great potential our Father has placed in me as well as how much he is continuously revealing to me on a daily basis. Even now he is showing me that there is a champion stored inside of me and that he is releasing me to the world in order to demonstrate to others what it means to be a champion. It is my prayer that your eyes of understanding have not only been opened but broadened into what God has patterned for you to accomplish in your lifetime and that you are an over-comer in Christ Jesus.

Therefore, I resolve that the destiny that is on my life is to encourage others while utilizing biblical principles, the struggles and the many tests that God has seen me through, that there is a great promise resting over my life, just as there is a great promise on your life.

CHAPTER EIGHT

A Champion is Born

"All who are victorious will inherit all these blessings, and I will be their God, and they will be my children"
Rev 21:7 (NLT)

Before any athlete becomes a champion prize winner or a star player, they first must endure many hours of rigorous training. There are various reasons as to why any athlete in any given sport participates in intensive training. One rationale stems from the fact that there is no coach in the sports field who would allow their athlete to begin at an upper level division in their respective sport unless they have proven they have the necessary skills, understand the fundamentals of the sport, and have been properly conditioned to challenge their opponent. Secondly, coaches want to see what potential the individual athlete possesses, if they have the heart for the sport and the willingness to undergo long hours of training until they reach championship status. Thusly, as an athlete improves their skill set the more they are elevated and recognized in the particular sport they play.

The same holds true for the children of God. As mentioned before the various tests we encounter throughout our life are not intended to kill us but to improve us, and better prepare us for the next test that will come along. Just like a boxer or sports player, the more we are placed in training the better we become as Christians and the more we are equipped to minister to others who maybe in the same predicament that we were just delivered from. It is preposterous to think that God would send anyone into the mission fields to gain souls for his kingdom if they had never experienced anything. In essence, tests are the training ground for our faith which in turn only increases our level of faith, builds character and uncovers how we as Christians should react to adversity or conflict when it occurs in our life.

Prior to gaining the revelation from the Holy Spirit that I had the victory, I had to endure a long season of training and preparation. During this time period God revealed to me the layers of pain, disappointment and un-forgiveness that was harboring in my heart and spirit that needed to be removed. God had to pull those layers away from me so that the calling that he placed on my life would not be corrupted or contaminated. The process of eradicating the corruptible layers that were dwelling in my spirit began when God assigned me to a meticulous spiritual workout. This spiritual workout consisted of a heart transplant, an attitude adjustment coupled with a series of tests and trials.

Changes in my heart condition did not take place until I acknowledged Jesus Christ as my Lord and savior, welcomed him into my life and gave him total control over my life. Before Christ came into my life the internal and external components of my spiritual being closely resembled that of an onion. When you think of an onion it has an outer layer for protection, nothing can permeate or break through it but when you peel the various layers back you get a clear picture of its composition.[3] No matter if you are working with a white onion or a sweet onion the more you pull back each layer the stronger or the sweeter the aroma gets.

Metaphorically speaking, the layers of an onion represent each of the hidden issues in our life down to the root causes of our dysfunction. In retrospect, when bad things happen to us we tend to allow those events to dictate to us who we will and will not trust; sometimes to the point we won't even trust God. This is the point where we view every situation in our life and everything around us from a negative perspective. The characteristics of a person with this behavior closely resemble the potency of a white onion, giving off an unpleasant odor. There's a tendency that a person of this nature is seldom pleasant to be around. A sweet onion on the other hand has all the same qualities of a white onion the only difference is the smell it gives off.

As a result, when God tears down the barriers that hinder us from being fully transformed he allows us to be tested in such a way that we don't have a choice but to confront and deal with the issues that were secretly concealed within our spirit. As God exposed each hidden layer of my distrust for people, I had to address the skepticism I had for those I was in relationship with and the new people who attempted to form a relationship with me. I had to stop thinking that everyone around me had an alternative motive or agenda. Now, I allow the spirit of discernment from the Holy Spirit to be my indicator of someone's intention for forming a relationship with me. Simply stated *I give people the benefit of doubt.*

At the same time that God was reconditioning my heart, he also changed my perspective of the world. This transformation happened when I had an *Aha* moment in the presence of the Lord. I had to realize that I was not the center of the universe and that the world did not revolve around me. I could no longer be self-centered or cynical toward those around me. I had to become part of the solution and not part of the problem. I had to come the point where I owned my reality and became more accountable for my actions and behavior. No longer could I blame anyone else for my misfortunate's in life, not even God. For the most part, I had to learn that my failure to forgive others for what they did to me contributed to the pain and disappointment I was carrying around. Until I forgave those who hurt me and acknowledged that I too may have hurt them by word or deed, I would never be able to break free and be made whole.

Earlier, an illustration of a boxer and sports player was discussed. When these individuals learn a new technique in training their trainers or coaches require them to perform the same technique during a mock practice drill so that they can see what area needs improvement. This same thing happened to me while going through God's reconstruction regimen of my heart and mind. However, he amplified the level of testing of my faith. There were times when situations would come out of the blue, where people would say and do things that would get on my nerves but I had to be ever so careful of how I responded because I knew I was not the same person anymore and if I did not pass the test the first time I would be required to take it again. Moreover, with each retest the greater the testing would be.

I believe that God wanted to make sure that the reformation of my heart and mind did not need any more refinement. Please do not misunderstand what I am saying I am not perfect I am still a work in progress. Nonetheless, an athlete would never know the level of their capabilities if they were not properly trained, pushed to their limit and challenged in the ring, on the field or the court.

Amazingly, we never know what is embedded in us or how great we are until we have been tried in the fire.

For a better portrayal of training, let's look at the life of David who was anointed at a young age by Samuel to one day replace Saul and become the king of Israel. Despite the fact that David had the capability to take down Goliath with a slingshot and a stone as a child, God knew David was too young and inexperienced to be a leader of a nation. Over his lifetime David was confronted with a multitude of challenges and mistakes; which in turn help shape and develop his character and leadership skills as well as his will to serve God.

The challenges coupled with mishaps I am referring to include: David running away from Saul because of his ensuing jealously toward him because of God's promise to make David king of Israel (1 Samuel 18:1-16), the countless times Saul tried to kill him (1 Samuel 19:1-10), his adulterous affair with Bathsheba and the murder of her husband Uriah (2 Samuel 11:1-26), his failure to discipline Amnon for the rape of Tamar and Absalom for killing Amnon in retaliation of raping his sister (2 Samuel 13:1-19; 23-29), down to his disobedience toward God for taking a census of the people of Israel and Judah (2 Samuel 24:1-17).

From David's journey we can see that in spite of his failures and bad decisions God was with him and always sent people to provide corrective instruction as a means to rectify his ways. As stated in Hebrews 12:11,"*No discipline is enjoyable while it is happening –it's painful! But afterward there will be a peaceful vest for right living for those who are trained in this way."* As David transitioned from adolescence into adulthood toward the promise of being the king of Israel he had to learn some valuable lessons that were often painful but necessary in order for him to become the great leader he was in the end.

Likewise, as I stumbled through life and experienced various life transforming episodes that forced me to look at myself in the mirror and strive to become a better person I had to accept the corrective consequences that God sent my way. Apart from the correction I received from God, I knew that he loved me so much that he wanted me to gain godly characteristics and qualities that would help shape my new thought process and outlook on life.

Subsequently, of all the tests I've gone through thus far in life, God used each one of them to bring me to the place where I am today; a place of victory. Those challenges in my life included many years of struggling in my faith in God and his son Jesus Christ, my relationships with family members and friends. Also, my challenges included the setbacks and failures I experienced in my finances and the fulfillment of my hopes and dreams.

It is because of those challenges being listed on my resume of life that I have come to the realization that I am not just in a place of victory but I am truly living a victorious life and that there is great purpose to my life. As it is written in scripture, *"the Lord is my strength and my song; he has given me victory"* (Psalm 118:14, *NLT*). As a result of the struggles in my life (past and present) and the series of lessons that I learned along the way toward the mark of victory in Christ Jesus; I have been given a strong testimony of hope to share with others.

CHAPTER NINE

Lessons Learned Along the Way

*"People who accept discipline are on the pathway to life,
But those who ignore correction will go astray"
Proverbs 10:17 (NLT)*

From the time I decided to dedicate my life to God, I discovered that there were many sides to him that I did not have the vocabulary to articulate. It is one thing to say the name of the Lord our God but it is another to know him through the challenges we experience, it is from these experiences that we gain a full understanding as to why he is called by that particular name.

In Finding Him, I found that God placed me here on earth with a purpose and a plan. Just as it is stated in Jeremiah 29:11 (*NLT*), *"For I know the plans I have for you,"* says the Lord. *"They are plans for good not for disaster, to give you a future and a hope."*

In Finding Him, I found that I have a voice and I have something to say to a chosen generation. This fact finding is true for you as well. The something we have to say to the world stems from our testimony and what God has delivered us from. I know you have heard it before but I must say it again, *without a test there is no testimony*. With that being said, nothing I have experienced in my life was in vain and the very fact that I am still here and you are reading about my life's journey proves that God has a plan for my life.

It is amazing to me that there are so many people who are aimlessly walking around without a clue as to why they are here on Earth. If you want substantial evidence just turn on your television and in tune into the local news or log onto social media and look at what people are doing and saying; there is no substance behind their actions. Many of these people put their trust and hope into mankind and when they arrive at the end result they realize that humans cannot give them what they truly need. The word of the God in Proverbs 29:18 *(NLT)* states: *"Where there is no revelation, the people cast off restraint...,"* I can honestly say that I too use to be one of those individuals but as I grew older and wiser in Christ Jesus and the word of God, I learned that I could only trust him and him alone.

Henceforth, out of the trials and tests God has brought me through it was revealed to me that *In Finding Him*, I found according to Romans 8:37 that I am more than a conqueror in Christ Jesus. In his sweet, loving and kind voice God told me, *"my child I never intended for you to lose in life concerning your mind, your relationships, your finances, your dreams, your health, your peace nor your joy."* God also told me that everything I endured was just a test of my faith and he allowed the enemy to test me just like he did Job (Read Job 1-41).

At the end of Job's testing, which involved the lost of his children, property and health, times when he questioned God, the betrayal of his friends and the lack of support from his wife. God blessed Job with double, what he lost was no comparison to what he gained. There is one important thing that must be mentioned here and that is Job did not gain double for his trouble until he prayed for his friends (Job 42:10). You know without a shadow of doubt that you have grown and gained a level of spiritual maturity when you are able to pray for those who have persecuted you or inflicted pain on you.

In Finding Him, I found that I was wonderfully and marvelously made (Psalm 139: 14). I found that I could no longer hap hazardously give myself (my love, my soul, my time, my attention or my feelings) to any man who did not value my existence, and who was emotionally unavailable or unable to commit. I discovered that it was okay to be alone and that I would make it in life without a man. Since the divorce from my ex-husband in 2006, it has been the Holy Trinity (God the Father, Jesus Christ, and the Holy Spirit) and I.

Throughout the course of being single, I have learned so much about myself and who I was created to be. In living a single life I have learned that I have a great sense of humor, I am creative, talented and have a high-level of intelligence. Moreover, in being with myself I found that God loves me as if I was his only child, the apple of his eye. I found that I am a King's kid, a child of *El Elyon* (God of Most High) and that when he created me he broke the mold. You may be saying to yourself at this very moment that I am a bit arrogant but when God made you he broke the mold as well and there is absolutely no one else on Earth quite like you.

In Finding Him, I discovered that he wants the very best for me and that he fashioned a Boaz just for me; a man of God who is after God's own heart and truly understands the meaning of intimacy (in·tuh·muh·see), hence, *into to me*.[4] This person, whoever he maybe will totally be into me to include my mind, body, and soul; as I am into him, accepting of all of his shortcomings and flaws. Although, I am still standing on God's promise for my Boaz to come into my life I wait patiently and remain open and obedient to the spirit of God as he continues to develop me into a Proverbs 31 Woman of God.

In Finding Him, I found that I can do all things through Christ Jesus who strengthens me (Philippians 4:13, *NKJV*). Throughout my life I have encountered skeptics, people who either had a low level of thinking or no faith at all, and they tried their best to convince me that I would not make it in life nor succeed with the dreams I had in my spirit but *GOD*. As a testament, I was able to obtain a bachelor's degree despite the fact I had my eldest son during my senior year in college. I also was able to acquire a graduate degree, start a business, and attain a Doctoral Degree in spite of all the obstacles I had to face in raising two sons as a single parent.

With these hindrances came bankruptcy, being on public assistance, and eventually no transportation. There were times when I did not even have enough money to purchase the basic necessitates such as toiletries for my family. Regardless of what I had to suffer through to come to this point in my life, God showed himself strong and mighty. He allowed me to see that when I was weak I was really strong because I was leaning on his strength and not my own. In addition, God proved to me that he is an on time God. I do not regret any of the setbacks I experienced because they taught me how to solely rely on the Lord and believe that he would make a way out of no way. My philosophy to making it through difficult storms in life is that *if God can't turn my circumstance around then no one can*.

In Finding Him, I found that God's ways and thoughts were far greater and better than mine (Isaiah 55:8-9). There were periods in my life when I thought I had the solution to resolve an issue I was confronted with but my answer to the problem only made matters worse. Case in point, years prior to filing bankruptcy when I lived in the land of plastic city (i.e. credit cards), I had the misnomer that in order to get out of debt all I had to do was to transfer debt from one credit card onto another card that had a lower to no interest rate and pay off the transferred amount before the introductory zero interest rate period had expired. However, this method was not fruitful and I only sunk deeper and deeper into debt.

After years of living in the land of Lo-Debar and realizing that my way of handling finances was not producing any favorable results, I decided to seek God for his infinite wisdom on how to get out of debt. From a biblical perspective the term Lo-Debar means barrenness, desolation, and no hope.

The first thing God did in response to my prayer for debt cancellation was to get to the core of my disobedience in the area of tithes and offerings. Scripture explicates in Malachi 3:7-11 (NIV)............

Ever since the time of your forefathers you have turned away from my decrees and have not kept them. Return to me, and I will return to you," says the Lord Almighty. But you ask, "How are we to return?" Will a man rob God? Yet you rob me. But you ask, "How do we rob you?" In tithes and offerings, you are under a curse-the whole nation of you—because you are robbing me. Bring the whole tithe into the storehouse, that there may be food in my house. Test me in this says,"the Lord Almighty," and see if I will not throw open floodgates of heaven and pour out so much blessings that you will not have room enough for it.....says the Lord Almighty.

It is based on this biblical excerpt and the instructions, there within, that I received a revelation that the only way I was going to live a debt-free life was to give back to God what was rightfully his and ever since that time I have consistently given my tithes and offerings to my church where I am being spiritually feed.

Surprisingly, my obedience to our Lord and Savior paid off years later when one of America's largest banks filed a lawsuit against me because they could not locate my ex-husband. This is the point in time in my life that God proved himself, simultaneously, to be *Yahweh Nissi* (The Lord of my banner) and *Yahweh Shammah* (The Lord is there) to me. As Yahweh Nissi and Yahweh Shammah in my life, I found that God would help me, be with me and fight each and every one of my battles as long as I gave them to him (2 Chronicles 20:17).

The aforementioned lawsuit took a great toll on my mental state to the extent that I had sleepless nights and could barely eat. But God reminded me that the battle was not mine and the rationale for him teaching me the importance of tithing was going to reap a great harvest if I continued in my giving and didn't give up on my faith in him. After several months of fasting, praying, paying my tithes, sowing seed offerings, trusting and believing in God, the courts ruled on my behalf and I won the case.

As stated in Malachi 3:11b *(NIV)*, *"…..I will prevent pests from devouring your crops, and the vines in your fields will not cast their fruit,"* says the Lord Almighty. More than often, the battles we face in life are not like the one I just described but battles that take place deep within our thoughts or mindsets. These battles encompass: memories, negative self-perceptions and ideologies of how we think people view us. Needless to say, if you are currently battling thoughts in your mind and trying your best to live a life full of the spirit and not of the flesh, or whatever the case may be in your particular situation, let God, who is always omnipresent and forever ready to provide you with aide to fight for you. Hence, as the word of the Lord says in *1Peter 5:7 (NLT)*, *"Give all your worries and cares to God, for he cares about you."*

Despite the circumstances that we may face in our own personal life and when we feel that we have no way of escape *Yahweh Nissi* and *Yahweh Shammah* is with us even if we do not realize it. As I learned that God was the Lord of my banner and that he was with me down to the very moments when I came to the realization that people took me for granted and devalued the relationship they had with me. God was also with me every step I took along my journey throughout life and that he wanted me to be complete and lacking nothing. In essence, the battles I have faced so far in life are no comparison to the profound lessons I have learned since I began my walk with God and that is; as the head general of his army, he has the best arsenal to take down the enemies in our life.

In Finding Him, I witnessed that God is a protector *(Yahweh Sabaoth)* and that he will keep you safe from all dangers seen and unseen (Psalm 27:1). There were times in my life when God truly encircled a host of angels around me. For instance, during my freshman year in college some friends and I went to a homecoming party at a popular night club. While we were inside the club a fight ensued between a young lady and her boyfriend, and the club security informed all club goers that we had to stay inside until the conflict was resolved. After thirty minutes of waiting the security officers gave everyone the okay to leave the club if they wished to. Subsequently, the young lady who had the altercation with her boyfriend was still outside with a gun. When my friends and I exited the building and begin walking back to campus, a group of people suddenly ran pass us while at the same time one of my friends who was behind me pushed me down. Later, I found out that the young lady had mistaken me for the girl she suspected her boyfriend to have cheated with and had pointed the gun at the back of my head. This incident is just one of many events in my life that God knew what would happen and placed a hedge of protection around me.

As I reflect back on my life I realize that there were countless times when God keep me safe from situations that should have resulted in disease or death, but he had something great planned for me to fulfill in the Earth. As the old saying goes, *God takes care of fools and babies*. Please don't get me wrong, I am not saying that I was a fool but that was a season when I was a bit green or should I say naïve. Remarkably enough, I am sure there are instances that you would like to forget of how God keep you safe and covered you in such a way that no one found out what he keep you safe from.

In Finding Him, I found that there is no condemnation for those who belong to Christ Jesus (Romans 8:1). In my quest to live a life that was holy and blameless before God I found that he was and is *Yahweh Tsidkenu*, the Lord our righteousness (Jeremiah 23:6). In comparison to the righteousness of Jesus Christ, I deduce that there is nothing I could ever do in life to make myself qualified to be saved. I can't be nice enough, give enough and not even dress holy enough to be saved.

In all honesty, I did not get to know God as *Yahweh Tsidkenu* until I came to my end, when I had no one to turn to and nothing else to hold on to. I got to a place where I had to come to terms with my sins. Earlier, I mentioned that I went through some trying times with my ex-husband; however, everything we went through was not totally his fault. Please do not misconstrue what I have shared with you about what I went through with my ex-husband as a character assassination against him but I am simply telling you what I have gone through in my life while in that relationship.

Now that I have been saved and washed clean by the blood of Jesus Christ, I can admit that I played a role in the demise of our marriage. As I look back on those times I was not a very nice person to live with and the words I spoke were not quite pleasant. It was mentioned in earlier chapters that, *"The tongue can bring death or life, those who love to talk will reap the consequences"* (Proverbs 18:21, NLT). This verse of scripture is true for the simple fact that whenever we got into an argument I said I wanted a divorce and over time the very thing I did not want to happen happened. We must be very careful of the words we speak into the atmosphere, especially if we are speaking out of anger.

Nonetheless, through God's grace, mercy and redemptive power I was given another chance to live a life that was pleasing unto him when I repented, confessed my sins, and asked the Savior for forgiveness. I am so glad that God is a god of many chances and grants us the opportunity to get it right with him. More than that, I am happy that the punishment that I rightfully deserve, the Lord Jesus Christ paid for them all on Calvary (2 Corinthians 5:21).

In Finding Him, I found that God is *Jehovah-rapha* the Lord who heals (Exodus 15:26). It is one thing to hear about God being a healer but it is another to know him from a personal standpoint. I learned firsthand that God is a healer in 2005 when I fell ill and nearly died. Although, it has been many years since that event has occurred I still give God all the glory and honor that he healed my body and allowed me to experience sickness because it prepared me to be a more effective witness of God's healing power and what he can do for believers and unbelievers, alike.

There are countless accounts throughout the bible where Jesus miraculously healed people of incurable diseases. For instance, think about the woman with the issue of blood (Matthew 9:18-22, NLT). There is no reference in the bible of this woman's name or occupation but what we do know is that she had a bleeding problem for twelve years that no amount of money could solve and there was no human knowledge available that could give her what she desired the most and that was to be healed. However, there was Jesus.

As indicated in Matthew 9:18-22, Jesus was on his way to the house of a synagogue leader who had asked him to go with him to his house and bring his dead daughter back to life. On his way to the leader's house Jesus was making his way through a crowd that was assembled outside of the synagogue and while walking someone touched him. The touch Jesus felt was from the woman who believed that if she could just simply touch him she would be healed. At the very moment that Jesus realized who had touched him, he turned around and saw the woman and said to her:"*daughter, be encouraged! Your faith has made you well."*

Another illustration in the bible where Jesus' healing power was experienced was in the lives of the man who had leprosy and the man who was paralyzed. In both instances, Jesus healed these men of their infirmities (Mark 1:40-44; Mark 2:1-12). Beyond the scope of healing people physically, God has the ability to not only regulate our minds but also our hearts. Right now, I should be walking around out of my mind after the miscarriage of my third child, but God saw it fit to stabilize my mind so that I could do his will.

Scripture states in Ephesians 4:23 *(NLT),"...let the Spirit renew your thoughts and attitudes."* Based on this scripture we should remember that the illness we or our love ones face in life is ultimately for the glory of God (John 9:1-3, *NLT)*. Like so, when man says there is no hope, there is nothing further that can be done medically God can and God will step in and do a supernatural work. We as children of the Most High must continue to trust and believe God's report above all others, along with maintaining our faith in his word.

In Finding Him, I found that God will truly supply all of my needs according to his riches in glory (Philippians 4:19). Whatever problem we have God has the answer to it. As *Yahweh Yireh (a.k.a* Jehovah jireh*)* the Lord will provide; God will provide the means to pay your bills if you are unemployed or underemployed by sending unexpected financial blessings. God always has a marvelous way of giving us exactly what we need when we need it. Just like he did when he tested Abraham in Genesis 22:1-14; from the text we gather that God wanted Abraham to sacrifice his only son Isaac in whom he loved very much. In his obedience Abraham followed God's instructions to go the land of Moriah to give Isaac as a burnt offering.

After several days of traveling Abraham with two of his servants and his son, finally arrived at the place where he was to sacrifice Isaac. The moment Abraham and his companions arrived at the indicated location, he told his servants that he and Isaac were going further into the land and they were to remain where they were. When Isaac and Abraham reached their destination, Isaac asked his father, *"Where is the sheep we will use for the burnt offering?"* Abraham responded to Isaac by saying, *"God would provide one."*

In preparation of the burnt offering Abraham built an altar and placed wood underneath it. Then Abraham tied Isaac down on the altar, at which time he picked up a knife to kill his son but before Abraham was able to bring the knife on Isaac an angel of the Lord called him by name. The voice told Abraham not to harm Isaac and because of his love for the Father, a ram was provided for the sacrifice. In either case of God being *Jehovah-rapha* or *Yahweh Yireh* he required both martyr's to have faith that did not waiver (James 1:6).

In Finding Him, I found that God is *El Roi* (the All Seeing and Knowing One). Because of God's omniscience there is nothing that we can do in life that God does not see or does not know. In life we often think that we can outsmart God and hide our dirty deeds and thoughts from him. David thought the same thing when he lusted after Uriah's wife Bathsheba. As a result of his lustful desire for another man's wife, David committed adultery, impregnated her and attempted to cover up his sin by having Uriah killed during battle (2 Samuel 11:1-27).

In spite of his efforts to hide his actions, God already knew what David had done and sent a messenger by the name of Nathan a prophet to rebuke him (2 Samuel 12:1-12). The story about David and Bathsheba serves as a prime example that no matter what we do to conceal our actions God already knows about them. Therefore, as it is stated in Proverbs 5:21 *NLT*, *"For the Lord clearly sees what a man does, examining every path he takes."*

On the other side of the pendulum, there is nothing we experience in life that catches God off guard. As an all seeing and knowing God, he knows when we are facing financial hardships, contending with an illness, or dealing with conflict on the job and at home. Whatever it maybe, God knows what we are confronted with and cares so much for us that he will make sure that we have the wisdom, knowledge and access to the tools we need to get us through our ordeal.

Even so, in my darkest hour and in times of desperation I found that God would never leave me nor forsake me (Hebrews 13:5). Oftentimes in my life I felt like I had no one to turn to, to tell my deepest and innermost thoughts to. I found that God was and still is that secret place where I can run to and find comfort and solace. I am so thankful and grateful to God that he is not like man. Once you tell him something you can be confident that you will never hear it again. This is the point in my Christian walk that God revealed himself as *Yahweh Shalom* (The Lord is Peace).

In the midst of me discovering God as Yahweh Shalom, I realized that he would give me peace that goes beyond my level of intellect or what I could ever fathom. The type of peace I am referring to is not like anything in this world. For example, you could have just received the most devastating news about a family member or just lost all of your worldly possessions but within your spirit you remain calm knowing that God has you covered.

In addition, to God revealing himself to me as Jehovah-Shalom, he taught me that he would be *Adonai* in my life as well. Kay Arthur, the author of *The Peace & Power of Knowing God's Name,* suggest that before anyone can acknowledge God as El Shaddai they first must recognize him as Adonai (Lord and Master); as well as acknowledge his lordship over their life by bowing before him.[5] Mrs. Arthur further explains that verbally recognizing God as Adonai is not something that a believer merely does, but they do so by forming a covenant relationship with him.[6]

My point, however, of coming into a relationship with God as Adonai (The Lord) occurred when I had a one-on-one encounter with him. This face-to-face encounter came as a result when I had exhausted all of life's options and I had nowhere else to turn to but to God. I had to make a conscious decision that I was either going to willingly surrender to God and allow him to rule over my life or keep living the way I was. I am glad to say that this decision came without hesitation because I made so many chooses that were not favorable or fruitful.

Most importantly, my willingness to follow God conveyed to him that I valued him and what he wanted for my life verses that which I desired. There will come a time in everyone's life when they will have to make the choice I did to follow Jesus Christ and to make him the focal point of their life; at which time they will discover him for themselves' to be Adonai.

In Finding Him, I found God to be *El Shaddai* (the God Almighty- the All Sufficient One) in my life (Genesis 17:1; Exodus 6:3). As the almighty creator *Elohim*, God will be whatever you need him to be in your time of trouble. God will be a father to the fatherless. He will be a friend to the friendless. God will hold your hand through the death of a husband, parent or child. He will be with you at your most vulnerable period in life, when you feel like you cannot make it anymore and you have no one to turn to for comfort.

I am a living witness to this fact because shortly after miscarrying and my ex-husband informing me that he wanted a divorce, I contemplated suicide. However, through God's love and compassion for me he sent angels to rescue me at the right moment and to whisper in my ear that he would be the love of my life if I would just surrender and trust him. From this experience the El Shaddai of my life became more than my savior but a friend and a comforter.

Furthermore, in *Finding Him* I found that as El Shaddai, God will give you a new name and identity; just like when he made a covenant with Abram informing him that he would be a father to many and he switched Abram's name to Abraham (Genesis17:1-6, NLT). After being saved for a number of years, I have become aware that not only did my name and identity change but my whole outlook on life. As a result of the change in my identity and name, I no longer view life as a routine: going to work, paying bills, raising children but a life that is more inclusive of serving God, ministering to others and inspiring them to reach their fullest potential in life.

During my season of being processed I gained a closer relationship with God, a stronger prayer life, an authentic praise, a greater testimony, Christ-like qualities, wisdom, spiritual maturity, a resilient spirit and a confident hope of salvation. *In Finding Him*, I found that the obstacles I faced in life were merely tests. The trials and challenges we all face are like the proverbial ring-around the roses of life. You get over one huddler and then another one comes along but there is one thing you can count on throughout these challenges and that is God.

Throughout many of my adversities God moved me from faith to faith and from glory to glory. Out of each of my tests and trials, I learned something new about God and myself that I did not know before. I witnessed certain aspects of God's character and discovered the different names that he is often referred to and what he will do in your life. Alongside the names I've previously described God to have been in my life, he's been *Yahweh* (The Self-Existent One). I am overwhelmed by the number of names of God

I experienced in my life and there are still sides to him that I have yet to encounter. All the way through my description of my journey with our Heavenly Father you will notice that it was not God who was lost but in fact it was I and the story continues until he says well done my good and faithful servant WELL DONE!

As I conclude the first portion of my testimony and the season of preparation, I have one question for you: *Are you ready to discover who you were truly made to be, regardless of the fact that you may have been betrayed, deceived, physically or emotionally abused, sexually assaulted, or whatever unimaginable experience you have endured in life?* If your answer is yes, then know this beloved that no matter what you had to endure (the good, the bad or the ugly) God has a wonderful way of turning mess into blessings. Scripture tells us in Romans 28:8 *(NLT)*, *"And we know that in all things God works for the good of those who love him, who have been called according to his purpose."* What you must understand and remember is that if we call ourselves the sons and daughters of the Most High, we must keep our faith in God and his word no matter what or how our circumstance may appear during the test.

Many times those who become born again in Christ Jesus have a tendency to believe that all of life's issues and problems will end but unfortunately that's not the case. As long as you or I live, we will have an assortment of trials that will come into our sphere to test our faith and whenever those tests come upon us we must say to ourselves, *"It's just a test of my faith!"* Bishop Victor T. Curry of New Birth Church Baptist Cathedral of Faith International said it best," *a faith that has not been tested is a faith that cannot be trusted."* [7]

Nonetheless, my battle scars are an indication that I made it through the tests and trials that I had to endure in order to reshape my mood of thinking; construct Godly character, leaven a spirit of perseverance and erase any sign of hurt or pain. Therefore, be reassured that God had a plan and has a plan and purpose for whatever you had to suffer through or those things you are going through right now in your life. What more can be said, than we are conquerors and winners in CHRIST JESUS!!

CHAPTER TEN

Author's Prayer

"Confess your sins to each other and pray for each other so that you may be healed….."
James 5:16 (NLT)

Over my life I have said and done something's that I am not proud of but being that God is sovereign, he was always waiting patiently to extend his love, grace and mercy toward me. Now he awaits you, will you accept him and welcome him into your life today? If you answered *yes*, then pray this prayer with me,

"Lord Jesus, I confess today that you died on Calvary and rose up so that I may have eternal life. I proclaim that you are the Son of the true living God and the redeemer of my soul. I ask that you come into my life today, forgive me of my sins, create in me a pure heart and renewed steadfast spirit." (Romans 10:9-10, Romans 12:2, Revelation 3:20, Psalms 51:10)

Welcome to the body of Christ and with your confession of faith you will now begin a new walk in life. You will accomplish things in your life that you never fathomed. You will go places you never thought you would have the opportunity to visit and meet people you never thought you would meet. Please do not be discouraged but now that you have switched teams and have accepted Christ into your life you will experience trials of many kinds.

As it is stated in 1Peter 1:7, *NLT*:

> *These trials will show that your faith is genuine. It is being tested as fire tests and purifies gold-though, your faith is far more precious than mere gold. So when your faith remains strong through many trials, it will bring you much praise and glory and honor on the day when Jesus Christ is revealed to the whole world.*

Here's my prayer to cover you as you transition into this new journey and walk in life:

*Father God, I pray that you will restore to my brother or sister the years that the locust ate up. -**Joel 2:25 NIV***

Lord Jesus, that you will make them the head and not the tail. ***-Deuteronomy 28:13 NIV***

May the Lord bless those who bless you and curse those who may curse you.- ***Genesis 12:3 NIV***

*May you forget the former things of your life and do not dwell on them. -**Isaiah 43:18 NIV***

*May you leave those things which are familiar and grasp hold to God and his plan for your life. -**Acts 7:2-3; Hebrews 11:8 NIV***

*May you take your position, stand firm and see the deliverance the Lord will give you. -**2 Chronicles 20:17 NIV***

May you be endowed to see things that your eyes have never seen, by Christ's spirit, that you will hear things you never heard before and that

Author's Prayer

your mind may conceive what God has prepared for you because you love Him. -**1 Corinthians 2:9**

May you call upon the Lord and He answers you and tells you great and unsearchable things you did not know. -***Jeremiah 33:3 NIV***

May grace and peace be yours in abundance through your new found knowledge of God the Father and His Son Jesus Christ our Lord. -**2 Peter 1:2**

May you go forward in this new walk of life with an attitude like Christ, showing forth humility and obedience. -**Philippians 2:5, 8**

May you grow as Jesus grew in wisdom and stature and in favor with God and man. -**Luke 2:52**

May you know that you were fearfully and wonderfully made (**Psalms 139:14 NIV**) and that you can do all things through Jesus Christ who gives you strength. -**Philippians 4:13 NIV**

May you be reassured that even when you face trials of many kinds that you will develop a spirit of perseverance. That this spirit of perseverance will lead you to be matured and complete in Christ Jesus and you will not lack anything. -***James 1:3-4 NIV***

For this reason, according to Colossians 1:9-13 NIV, since the day the Body of Christ has heard about you, we have not stopped praying for you and asking God to fill you with the knowledge of his will through all spiritual wisdom and understanding. And we pray this in order that you may live a life worthy of the Lord and may please him in every way bearing fruit in every good work, growing in the knowledge of God, being strengthened with all power according to his glorious might, so that you may have great endurance and patience, and joyfully giving thanks to the Father, who has qualified you to share in the inheritance of the saints in the kingdom of light. For he has rescued you from the dominion of *darkness and brought you into the kingdom of the Son he loves, in whom you have redemption, the forgiveness of sins.* -Amen

Now that you have made this commitment to be in the kingdom of God, make sure that you connect with a bible teaching church that will further equip you with the word of God, so that you may fulfill the destiny that is on your life.

Amazed by His Grace and Love!

… SPIRITUAL GROWTH GUIDE FOR CHANGE

Appendix A

SPIRITUAL GROWTH GUIDE FOR CHANGE

This section has been provided to assist you in your new found walk with Jesus Christ. The following questions are only suggestions and serve as a means to help you shape an individualized spiritual growth plan for change. You have the option to add or delete anything as you see fit and as it relates to your plan to grow spiritually. Additional pages have been provided for areas not already covered.

SELF-DISCOVERY

Reference scriptures: Jeremiah 29:11; Romans 16:25; Eph. 3:9; 2 Tim. 1:9; John 1:3; 2 Thessalonians 1:11-12; Titus 1:1

For what purpose was I born?

_____

_____

_____

_____

_____

_____

What gifts and talents do I possess that God can use to fulfill his purpose?

_____

_____

_____

_____

_____

_____

How do my plans for life align with the will of God and his plans for me?

_____

_____

_____

_____

_____

_____

How do I view myself and the life I have lived and desire to live?

_____

_____

_____

_____

SPIRITUALITY

Reference scriptures: Romans 4:20-21, 10:17; Galatians 3:2, 5; Colossians 3:16; Luke 17:6; Acts 2:42; Ephesians 3:19; Hebrews 10:25; Malachi 3:8-11

Why is it important for me to develop a personal relationship with Jesus Christ?

_____

_____

_____

_____

_____

_____

How can I establish a personal relationship with Jesus Christ?

_____

_____

_____

_____

_____

_____

_____

_____

In what ways can I build my faith in God?

_____

_____

_____

_____

_____

_____

In what ways can I grow in the wisdom and knowledge of God?

_____

_____

_____

_____

_____

_____

Why is it important for me to fellowship with other believers?

_____

_____

_____

_____

_____

_____

How can I help with the expansion of God's kingdom?

_____
_____
_____
_____
_____
_____

How does giving of tithes and offering connect with my relationship with God?

_____
_____
_____
_____
_____
_____

How does giving back to God increase my faith and the goal of helping others?

_____
_____
_____
_____

FORGIVENESS

Reference scriptures: Colossians 3:13-15; Matt. 6:15; Luke 6:37, 11: 4; 17:3-4; Romans 12:17-21

Why is it important to forgive those who have inflicted pain on me?

___

___

___

___

___

___

In what ways have I forgiven others?

___

___

___

___

___

___

___

___

How can I move beyond the hurt of my past and live a well-rounded life?

Appendix B

Personal Questions for Growth and Change

My person growth question about family:

_____

_____

Answer/Revelation:

_____

_____

My personal growth question about love:

_____

_____

Answer/Revelation:

_____

_____

Personal Questions for Growth and Change

My personal growth question about relationships:

_____

_____

_____

Answer/Revelation:

_____

_____

_____

My personal growth question about my future:

_____

_____

_____

Answer/Revelation:

_____

_____

_____

Personal Questions for Growth and Change

My personal growth question about my finances:

_____

_____

_____

Answer/Revelation:

_____

_____

_____

My personal growth question about my health:

_____

_____

_____

Answer/Revelation:

_____

_____

_____

Personal Questions for Growth and Change

My personal growth question about my hopes and dreams:

_____

_____

_____

Answer/Revelation:

_____

_____

_____

My personal growth question of how to give back to my community:

_____

_____

_____

Answer/Revelation:

_____

_____

_____

Endnotes

[1] Geoffrey Nunberg. "Kindness,"*The American Heritage College Dictionary* (New York: Houghton Mifflin Company, 1993), 747.

[2] Ibid., 752, 1548.

[3] John D. Casnig, "The Seven Veils of an Onion," *A Language of Metaphors.* Accessed February 4, 2016, http://www.knowgramming.com/Onion.htm

[4] "*Intimacy,*" Dictionary.com Unabridged, accessed March 25, 2016, http://www.dictionary.com/browse/intimacy

[5] Kay Arthur, *The Peace and Power of Knowing God's Name* (Colorado: Water Brook Press, 2002), 48.

[6] Ibid., 49.

[7] Victor T. Curry, *"Faith on Trial,"* (sermon presentation, New Birth Missionary Baptist Church, Lithonia, GA, September 25, 2016; September 8, 2013).

Ways to Keep in Contact with Author

To correspond with Dr. Bessie Stewart-Banks
send all inquiries to bessieban27@gmail.com
or

c/o Conscious of the Heart Publishing, LLC
P.O. Box 1452
Redan, Georgia 30074
For book title promotional products email: information
request @conscious.oftheheart@gmail.com

www.ingramcontent.com/pod-product-compliance
Lightning Source LLC
Chambersburg PA
CBHW050651160426
43194CB00010B/1900